healthy
food
for kids

healthy food for kids

quick recipes for busy parents

RACHAEL ANNE HILL

PHOTOGRAPHY BY NOEL MURPHY

RYLAND
PETERS
& SMALL

LONDON NEW YORK

Senior Designer Anna Murphy
Editor Sharon Cochrane
Picture Research Tracy Ogino
Production Patricia Harrington
Art Director Gabriella Le Grazie
Publishing Director Alison Starling

Food Stylist Joss Herd
Assistant Food Stylist Harry Eastwood
Stylist Chloe Brown
Recipe Development and Testing Gina Steer
Index Hilary Bird

First published in the United States in 2005
by Ryland Peters & Small, Inc.
519 Broadway, 5th Floor
New York, NY 10012
www.rylandpeters.com

10 9 8 7 6 5 4 3 2 1

Library of Congress Cataloging-in-Publication Data

Hill, Rachael Anne.
  Healthy food for kids / Rachael Anne Hill ; photography by Noel Murphy.
    p. cm.
  Includes index.
  ISBN 1-84172-814-4
  1. Cookery, American. 2. Quick and easy cookery. 3. Children--Nutrition. I. Title.
  TX715.H685 2005
  641.5973--dc22

                                           2005006114

Printed in China

Notes

All spoon measurements are level unless otherwise specified.

Ovens should be preheated to the specified temperature. If using a convection oven, cooking times should be reduced according to the manufacturer's instructions.

All eggs are medium unless otherwise specified. I recommend using free-range, organic eggs where possible. Uncooked or partly cooked eggs should not be served to the very young, the very old, pregnant women, or to those with compromised immune systems.

All fruit and vegetables should be washed thoroughly.

Whole nuts should not be served to children under the age of five because of the risk of choking. Always chop nuts or grind them finely.

Honey should not be served to children under 12 months of age.

To sterilize preserving jars, wash them in hot, soapy water and rinse in boiling water. Place them in a large saucepan and cover with hot water. With the saucepan lid on, bring the water to a boil and continue boiling for 15 minutes. Turn off the heat, leaving the jars in the hot water until just before they are to be filled. Drain and dry the jars. Sterilize the lids by boiling them for 5 minutes or according to the manufacturer's instructions. Jars should be filled and sealed while they are still hot.

CONTENTS

YOUR CHILD'S DIET

WHAT'S THE PROBLEM?

All parents want the best for their children and naturally want them to be fit and healthy. The building blocks of good health begin with a nutritious, balanced diet, so no parent would intentionally feed their child unhealthy foods and yet, according to recent figures, the following is true:

92% of children have intakes of saturated fat that exceed the maximum recommended level for adults

83% of children eat more added sugars than the maximum recommended level for adults

the average child eats **less than half** the recommended amount of fruit and vegetables per day

over 50% of all children eat twice as much salt as they should

the average child eats **over 80** food additives a day

WHY ARE KIDS EATING SUCH UNHEALTHY DIETS?

Over the past 20 to 30 years, freshly prepared, home-cooked food has gradually been replaced by commercial, ready-made alternatives. So much so that large numbers of children today are eating a diet that consists almost entirely of foods that have been prepared outside the home—from breakfast cereals and snacks to their evening meal. While there is no denying the convenience of feeding our children in this way, the fact remains that the companies preparing these foods are primarily in business to create healthy profits, not healthy children.

In theory, these two objectives are not mutually exclusive, but a closer inspection of the vast majority of commercially prepared foods, especially those targeted specifically at children, shows that they are rarely achieved in tandem. Most of these foods are made from poor-quality ingredients, are low in nutrients, high in saturated fat, salt, and sugar, bulked out with cheap fillers, colored, flavored to mask poor taste, and full of preservatives.

A recent survey of over 400 so-called "child-friendly" foods found evidence of very high levels of fat, salt, and sugar. They were also shown to contain an average of five additives—with some as many as 16—some of which are known to cause temper tantrums, lack of concentration, excessive fidgeting, interrupting, hyperactivity, an inability to sleep, and bed wetting in 25 percent of all young children. More than one-third of the products contained colorings, including Azo dyes—known to be linked to hyperactivity, asthma, and rashes, while over 75 percent had flavorings, including monosodium glutamate, guanosine, and sodium 5'-ribonucleotide that can cause rashes, lack of concentration, and hyperactivity.

DON'T BELIEVE THE HYPE

The true nutritional quality of foods marketed specifically at children is all too often hidden behind poorly labeled, brightly colored packaging and reassuring—but often highly misleading—health claims. Millions of dollars are spent on television advertisements for these products, strategically placed between both our own and our kids' favorite shows, with the intention of convincing us that these products are healthier, tastier, and more desirable than they really are.

So successful has this marketing been that almost every kitchen is stocked full of ready-prepared food. Likewise, kids' lunch boxes are packed with potato chips, candy, sugar-laden cakes, and highly processed, "child-friendly" snacks—many of which are so nutritionally inferior they should carry a health warning.

COSTLY CONVENIENCE

In the last ten years alone, childhood obesity has increased by 300 percent. Incidences of cancer are increasing year on year, heart disease is our biggest killer, and type 2 diabetes—a disease traditionally only associated with adults—is now appearing in children as young as 12 years of age. A poor diet has been a large contributing factor towards these worrying statistics. In fact, the health consequences of eating a diet made up predominantly of nutritionally inferior foods are so profound that there have been cases where children are even failing to outlive their parents.

READY MEALS

With parents becoming busier and more ready meals and snacks appearing on the supermarket shelves, increasing numbers of children are hardly ever given the opportunity to eat home-cooked food made from fresh ingredients. On the rare occasions that they are given such food, their taste buds are so accustomed to the high fat, salt, and sugar content of the commercially prepared foods that they invariably reject it. This only serves to confirm our belief that kids actually "need" to eat over-processed, nutritionally inferior foods—a belief that has become so ingrained that our kids are routinely fed these foods not only by ourselves but by daycare centers, schools, and restaurants, too. This is why it is important to keep the amount of commercially prepared foods our children eat to a minimum from day one, which means weaning babies on home-cooked foods rather than on the often bland, artificial tasting, storebought jars.

This isn't to say that children can't be coaxed away from highly processed foods, it may just take a little longer. That's why this book is packed with all the kids' favorites. The difference is that not only will the burgers, fish sticks, and chicken nuggets you make taste a whole lot better than anything you can buy, they will also be far higher in protein, vitamins, and minerals, much lower in fat and salt, and totally additive-free. Also, when your children experience how good a real burger can taste, getting them to eat a healthier diet might be easier than you anticipated.

WHAT YOUR CHILDREN NEED FOR GOOD HEALTH

In order for children to get all the nutrients they need for healthy growth and development, they need a nutritious balanced diet. The easiest way to guarantee your children are getting all the nutrients they need is to provide as varied a diet as possible, based roughly on the food groups and proportions given below.

A BALANCED DIET

The diagram on the right shows the proportions of each type of food a child needs in order to get a healthy balanced diet— approximately one-third grains and potatoes, one-third fruit and vegetables, and one-third divided equally between protein- and calcium-rich foods. If your kids eat foods in these proportions, and a wide variety of each type of food, then they should be getting all the essential nutrients they need for good health.

You may be surprised to see a small segment is included for fatty, sugary foods. As long as the majority of your child's diet is made up of nutritious foods, it is okay to include these occasionally. It is important that no food is seen to be "banned" or "bad" otherwise your kids will award it forbidden fruit status and want to eat it the most.

protein-rich foods

fruit and vegetables

fatty and sugary foods

calcium-rich foods

grains and potatoes

GRAINS AND POTATOES

Starchy carbohydrates, such as bread, cereals, rice, pasta, potatoes, and legumes, are broken down by the body to form its main source of energy, glucose. Unfortunately, many carbohydrate-rich foods available today have

been highly refined, a process which not only strips them of much of their vitamin, mineral, and fiber content, but also increases the speed at which they release their sugars into the blood stream. The body is programmed to ensure that blood sugar levels remain relatively stable, so when we eat these fast-releasing sugars the body responds by secreting large amounts of the sugar-lowering hormone, insulin. As a result, the rising blood sugar levels plummet leaving us tired and listless. Children are particularly affected by fluctuating blood sugar levels and often show signs of fidgeting, hyperactivity, shouting, or aggression as levels surge, followed by tiredness, temper tantrums, and a lack of concentration as they fall.

This yo-yo effect can generally be avoided by replacing refined carbohydrates with unrefined ones, such as whole-wheat bread, whole-grain cereals, and whole-wheat pasta. These wholefood alternatives are not only broken down by the body more slowly, resulting in a more sustained release of energy, they are also far richer in fiber, B vitamins (needed for growth and energy), iron, magnesium, and immune-boosting zinc.

12 EASY WAYS TO INCREASE FRUIT AND VEGETABLE INTAKE

1 Puree vegetables to make soups or pasta sauces (pages 74, 86, and 89)

2 Puree fruits to make compotes (page 121) to be stirred into yogurt, oatmeal, custard, or ice cream, or spooned onto cereals and desserts

3 Make fresh fruit smoothies for breakfast, snacks, or dessert (page 42)

4 Make freshly squeezed fruit and vegetable juices (page 68)

5 Chop raw vegetables, such as bell peppers and celery, into sticks and serve as crudités for dips (page 48)

6 Make your own pizza and top it with a variety of vegetables, such as spinach, zucchini, and tomatoes (page 82)

7 Mash together a few boiled root vegetables, such as carrots, sweet potatoes, parsnips, and rutabagas, and serve this instead of mashed potato

8 Make your own vegetable burgers (page 109)

9 Make vegetable dippers out of root vegetables such as parsnips, sweet potatoes, or carrots (page 51)

10 Puree fresh fruit and freeze to make frozen pops (page 139) or use as a substitute for ice cream

11 Add extra vegetables to meals your children like, such as corn kernels and spinach to pasta sauces

12 Top breakfast cereals, ice cream, or yogurt with slices of fresh fruit

Did You Know?

The brain relies entirely on broken-down carbohydrates (glucose) to function, so when blood sugar levels fall, concentration levels and behavior are directly affected. This is just one more reason why slower-releasing carbohydrates are essential to your child's diet.

FRUIT AND VEGETABLES

Rich in vitamins and minerals, fruit and vegetables are also great sources of phytochemicals, which help to keep the immune system strong and protect against a whole host of illnesses and diseases. Rather than focusing on any one fruit or vegetable, try to include as many different colored ones as possible to ensure that your child gets a wide variety of nutrients.

PROTEIN-RICH FOODS

Essential for healthy growth and the development and repair of skin, muscle, and other tissues, protein is a vitally important part of a growing child's diet. Foods rich in protein include meat, poultry, fish, dairy products, eggs, nuts, seeds, beans, and legumes.

CALCIUM-RICH FOODS

The mineral calcium is important for building strong, healthy bones and teeth. Calcium-rich foods also provide several of the B vitamins, as well as vitamin A and D. Good sources of calcium include dairy products, eggs, canned sardines with bones, legumes, nuts, dried fruit, leafy green vegetables, tofu, and whole grains.

The saturated fat content of calcium-rich dairy foods can be reduced for children over the age of five by using low-fat versions of milk, yogurt, and cheese. However, children under five need the full-fat versions because they need the extra calories and vitamins that these provide.

ESSENTIAL FATTY ACIDS

Omega 3 and omega 6 fats, known as essential fatty acids, can't be made in the body so they must be supplied by the diet. They are vital for children's health as they help to boost the immune system, build healthy cells, and discourage allergies. Omega 6 fats are found in oils—such as safflower, sesame, sunflower, grapeseed, soy, and corn—nuts and seeds.

Omega 3 fats in particular are needed for healthy brain growth and development. In fact, recent research indicates that these fats may be so influential on the development of brain and central nervous tissue that a diet rich in them may result in fewer temper tantrums and an increased ability to concentrate, especially in kids who already have a history of attention deficit disorder and hyperactivity. Omega 3 fats are found in oily fish, such as mackerel, sardines, and salmon, leafy green vegetables, sweet potatoes, whole grains, beans, flaxseed, flaxseed oil, walnuts, walnut oil, canola oil, olives, and olive oil.

HOW TO ENSURE KIDS GET ALL THE ESSENTIAL FATTY ACIDS THEY NEED

Give oily fish, such as salmon, herring, sardines, or mackerel, to your children once or twice a week. Because oily fish can harbor harmful substances called dioxins, it is recommended that boys under 16 consume no more than four portions of oily fish a week and girls no more than two (this is because dioxin levels can accumulate in the body and may harm an unborn child in the future).

Encourage your children to snack on nuts and seeds and include them in breakfast cereals, cakes, and cookies, and sprinkle them over salads.

Spread peanut butter on toast.

Give kids plenty of fresh vegetables, especially leafy green varieties.

Use nut or seed oils in salad dressings.

HOW MUCH DO CHILDREN NEED TO EAT?

This chart is to be used as a guide only—some children will eat slightly more, some slightly less. Younger children usually need to eat slightly less than older ones so the exact size of a portion will vary, too.

FOOD GROUP	SERVINGS PER DAY	EXAMPLES OF A SERVING
grains and potatoes	4–6	**one serving is approximately the size of a child's fist, for example:** 1 slice of bread • 1 small bread roll • 3 to 4 tablespoons cooked pasta or rice • 2 to 3 tablespoons (1 oz.) breakfast cereal • a fist-sized potato or sweet potato • 2 crackers
vegetables	3	**one serving is approximately the amount a child can hold in one hand, for example:** 2–3 tablespoons (½ cup) raw or cooked vegetables • about 1 oz. raw leafy vegetables, such as spinach or lettuce • 1 medium tomato or 3–5 cherry tomatoes • 1 medium glass of vegetable juice (6 oz.)
fruit	2	**one serving is approximately the amount a child can hold in one hand, for example:** ½ grapefruit, mango, or papaya • 1 medium apple, pear, kiwi, satsuma, peach, banana, or plum • 2 to 3 tablespoons (½ cup) smaller fruits, such as grapes or berries • 2 to 3 tablespoons (½ cup) dried fruit • 2 to 3 tablespoons canned fruit • 1 medium glass of fruit juice (6 oz.)
calcium-rich foods	2	**one serving is approximately the size of a child's fist, for example:** 1 medium glass of milk (5 oz.) • 1 yogurt (3½ oz.) • a piece of cheese or tofu (about 1 oz.) • 1 to 2 tablespoons canned sardines
protein-rich foods	2	**one serving is approximately the size of a child's palm, for example:** 1 slice of lean meat (2 to 3 oz.) • 2 thin slices of chicken or turkey (2 to 3 oz.) • a piece of fish about half the size of a child's palm • 1 large egg • a small handful of nuts or seeds • 1 soy burger or sausage • ½ cup soy "meat" • ½ cup legumes

WHAT KIDS SHOULD AVOID

There are certain things that appear all-too-frequently in many processed foods that do our children more harm than good. Unfortunately, these unwanted elements are often found in even greater quantities in foods that are targeted specifically at our children. Here's what to avoid whenever you can.

TOO MUCH SALT

There is now overwhelming evidence to show that a diet high in salt leads to high blood pressure, stroke, and heart disease. It is also linked to an increased risk of osteoporosis and has been shown to aggravate asthma. Despite this, 50 percent of children are routinely consuming more than twice the recommended level of salt.

Children's high intake of salt is largely due to the amount of processed foods they are eating, most of which has salt added to it by the manufacturer. Also, foods specifically marketed at children, such as canned baked beans and pasta shapes, fish sticks and chicken nuggets, often have an even higher salt content than the adult versions.

AGE	MAXIMUM DAILY SALT INTAKE
up to 12 months	1,000 mg
1–6 years	2,000 mg
7–14 years	less than 5,000 mg

HOW TO CUT BACK

- Given that 75 to 80 percent of the salt we eat is hidden in processed foods, the most effective way to reduce salt intake is to cut back on these as much as possible and to replace them with fresh, natural alternatives. This is a particularly effective way of reducing the salt intake of kids because they generally eat a large amount of processed foods.
- Replace processed meats, such as salami, sausages, and burgers, with unsalted fish, fresh chicken, turkey, lamb, and beef.
- Replace processed cheeses, cheesy snacks, and feta cheese with cream cheese, natural cottage cheese, Cheddar, and mozzarella.
- Replace chips, salted nuts, and other salty snacks with unsalted mixed nuts, dried fruit, unsalted crackers, and raw vegetables.
- Replace canned foods, especially baked beans, canned pastas, and commercially prepared soups and sauces, with homemade alternatives.

FOOD	SALT PER CHILD SERVING
chicken nuggets	1,750 mg
pizza	1,250 mg
doughnut	1,200 mg
burger	2,000 mg
milk shake	500 mg
frosted cereal	1,500 mg

TOO MUCH SUGAR

Eighty-three percent of children eat more added sugars than the maximum level recommended for adults. Sugars come in many forms; they may be called sucrose, glucose, maltose, fructose, dextrose, glucose syrup, corn syrup, hydrolyzed starch, inverted sugar, or concentrated fruit juice. So when checking a food label for sugar, make sure you look for these "hidden" sugars, too.

The biggest known health problem caused by too much sugar in a child's diet is the appearance of dental caries. However, foods high in sugar are also often high in fat or alternatively low in essential nutrients, therefore they fill a child up with "empty calories," while leaving less room for other more nutritious foods. As a result, a diet high in sugar is often linked to poor nutritional intake and obesity. Ideally, only 10 percent of a child's daily calories should come from sugar in any form.

AGE	MAXIMUM DAILY SUGAR INTAKE
4–6 years	8 teaspoons
7–10 years	9 teaspoons
11+ years	10 teaspoons

HOW TO CUT BACK

- Check food labels for hidden sugars, such as sucrose, glucose, maltose, dextrose, lactose, syrup, corn syrup, hydrolyzed starch, inverted sugar, fructose, or concentrated fruit juice, and choose foods that contain less than 2 g sugar per 100 g.

- Only add sugar to food when necessary. Try sweetening foods in other ways, for example by adding dried fruit to cakes, or mashed bananas to plain yogurt.

- Homemade desserts are likely to contain much less added sugar than commercially made ones so make your own whenever possible. Alternatively, offer fresh or dried fruit, or canned fruit in its own juice.

- Replace sugary drinks with water, unsweetened fruit juice diluted with still or sparkling water, fresh fruit smoothies, and homemade juices (pages 42 and 68).

- Swap processed, sugary breakfast cereals for lower sugar alternatives, such as whole bran and whole-grain cereals, homemade muesli (page 32), and oatmeal.

- Keep high-sugar snacks like cookies and fruit bars to a minimum and replace them with homemade or savory alternatives (pages 60–67) or fresh fruit.

FOOD YOU LEAST EXPECT TO CONTAIN HIGH LEVELS OF SUGAR

FOOD	SUGAR
1 generous helping of commercially prepared tomato ketchup	1 teaspoon
1 child serving of baked beans	2½ teaspoons
1 small pot of flavored yogurt	up to 4 teaspoons
1 child serving of vanilla ice cream	3 teaspoons
1 child serving of canned corn	2 teaspoons

TOO MUCH SATURATED AND HYDROGENATED FAT

Saturated fat—found in meat, meat products, whole milk, hard cheese, butter, lard, and cream—raises blood cholesterol levels and increases the risk of heart disease and cancer. Like all fats, at 9 calories per gram, it is one of the most calorie dense nutrients and therefore increases the likelihood of obesity. Over 90 percent of children consume more saturated fat than the recommended level for adults.

Hydrogenated fats or trans fats are vegetable oils that have been artificially hardened during the manufacturing process. Manufacturers like to use them because they are cheap and can increase a food's shelf life. Consequently, they are often found in commercially prepared cakes, cookies, margarines, and desserts. However, this "new" fat has been shown to be even more harmful to the body than saturated fat because not only does it raise levels of "bad" cholesterol (as does saturated fat), but it also reduces levels of "good" cholesterol, therefore doubling the risk of heart disease. Recent food surveys have shown that foods specifically targeted at children are often particularly high in hydrogenated fats.

The amount of saturated and hydrogenated fat in your child's diet should be kept to a minimum. Ideally, these foods should make up no more than 10 percent of a child's daily calorie intake.

HOW TO CUT BACK

To reduce saturated fat:
- Cut back on cakes, cookies, potato chips, chocolate, ice cream, and processed foods, especially processed meats.

To reduce hydrogenated fat:
- Choose margarines and spreads that contain little or no hydrogenated fat (check the label).
- Bake your own cakes and cookies. Commercially prepared products contain the most trans fats of any food.
- Cut back on chips, ready-prepared snacks, and chocolate confectionery as much as possible, all of which can contain relatively high levels of hydrogenated fats.
- Avoid fast food because it is usually fried in partially hydrogenated oil.

MECHANICALLY SEPARATED MEAT

The meat residue that is left on the carcass of an animal after all the prime cuts have been removed is often pressure-blasted off the bones forming a reddish slurry. This is known as mechanically separated meat. Some food manufacturers use this as a cheap way to bulk up their meat products. It should be avoided because it contains fewer nutrients than prime cuts of meat.

HOW TO CUT BACK

- Mechanically separated meat must be labeled as "mechanically separated beef or pork," so always read the food label.

CHEAP FILLERS

Manufacturers often keep costs low by bulking out food with cheap fillers, such as maltodextrin, modified starch, starch, and modified cornflour, all of which have very little nutritional value. They just serve to fill up small tummies with "empty calories," leaving less room for more nutritious food.

HOW TO CUT BACK

- By cutting back on processed foods, such as cakes, cookies, chips, and other sugary and savory snacks, you will automatically cut back on cheap fillers such as these.

ADDITIVES

On average, we eat nearly eight pounds of food additives per person every year. The negative health effects of children consuming large amounts of additives has not been adequately researched. However, according to a recent study, some food additives could be responsible for excessive fiddling, interrupting, tantrums, lack of concentration, hyperactivity, and difficulty sleeping in up to 25 percent of all young children. If you feel there could be a connection between your children's behavior and their diet, exclude foods containing the suspect additives for a couple of weeks and see if you notice an improvement in behavior.

COLORINGS

Most artificial colorings are synthetic chemicals that don't occur in nature. The use of coloring usually indicates that no fruit or other natural ingredient has been used. As a result they appear most commonly in foods of low nutritional value, such as candy, sodas, jell-o, and desserts.

Colorings can also cause hyperactivity in some sensitive children. A recent U.K. government study has found that some artificial food colorings, including tartrazine (FD&C Yellow No. 5) and sunset yellow (FD&C Yellow No. 6), and the preservative sodium benzoate could be responsible for behavioral changes in children. These controversial dyes are likely to be used in products such as birthday cakes with brightly colored icings. However, many seemingly uncolored, harmless foods, such as canned fruit, may also contain these behavior-disrupting additives. Always check the food label and try to avoid them wherever possible.

FLAVORINGS, FLAVOR ENHANCERS, AND ARTIFICIAL SWEETENERS

The word "flavorings" can be used to describe more than 4,000 chemicals. Many are deemed to be safe, although a few can lead to intolerance in some children resulting in asthma, headaches, rashes, and eczema. Flavorings are most commonly used in products that are lacking in the real thing. Consequently, like colorings, they often appear in foods of poor nutritional value. Manufacturers often keep the identity of artificial (and natural) flavorings a secret, which can make it difficult to know exactly what you are feeding your children.

Artificial sweeteners are routinely used by manufacturers to flavor foods and drinks because they are even cheaper than sugar. They are less harmful to children's teeth, but they still condition their taste buds into liking intensely sweet foods. Officially, they are deemed to be safe, however tests linking high intakes with increased incidences of cancer and neurological problems has left a question mark hanging over just how safe they are.

PRESERVATIVES

Manufacturers use preservatives to extend the shelf life of foods. There are some natural preservatives available, such as natural acids and salts, but most of the commonly used preservatives are manufactured. The safety of their use in children's foods has not yet been proven, therefore they are best avoided wherever possible. It is known that certain preservatives, such as sulphur dioxide which is often used to stop discoloration in dried fruit, also destroy vitamin B1 and can cause adverse reactions, such as asthma attacks in susceptible children.

HOW TO CUT BACK

- The easiest and most effective way to reduce the number of additives your child consumes is to cut back on the amount of pre-prepared and processed foods they eat and replace them with fresh, natural, homemade alternatives. Only then will you know exactly what your child is consuming. Always read food labels carefully.

PESTICIDES

Exposure to pesticide residues in early life has been linked to a greater risk in later life of cancer, neurological impairment, and dysfunction of the immune, endocrine, and nervous systems. Children are more vulnerable to pesticide residues in food and drink because not only are their systems immature and in the process of developing, but weight for weight children consume far more of certain foods than adults. This is particularly true for a weaning baby who, weight for weight, will eat considerably more fruit and vegetables than an adult.

Consequently, the exposure of children and babies to pesticide residues is substantially underestimated. This was confirmed in 1998 when the U.S. Environmental Working Group reported that one in every 20 children consumes unsafe levels of organophosphate chemicals every day. A child also has a one-in-four chance of eating a peach with an unsafe dose of pesticides, a one-in-seven chance of eating an apple, and a one-in-eight chance of eating a nectarine with an unsafe dose. Many fruit and vegetables contain pesticide residues, but they are also found in products like breakfast cereals, cereal bars, and chips.

HOW TO CUT BACK

- Choose organic varieties of fruit and vegetables wherever possible (page 19). If possible, why not grow some of your own? You'll be amazed how readily a child will eat something he has grown himself.

ORGANIC FOODS

Children deserve the best possible food made from the safest, healthiest ingredients. Not only are their cells multiplying at their peak as their little bodies grow and their vital organs develop, but a child's kidneys are immature and therefore less able to filter out and break down harmful substances. In addition to this, their nervous systems are rapidly developing, a process that can be disrupted by exposure to toxins. Finally, weight for weight, children consume far higher proportions of many foods than adults.

It is for all these reasons that I recommend buying organic produce wherever availability and finances will allow, especially fruit, vegetables, meat, and dairy items. Organic foods are grown without the use of pesticides and chemicals. Animals reared organically will not have been routinely given hormones and antibiotics, so residues from these chemicals will not be found in their meat. You can also be assured that organic foods won't contain genetically modified ingredients, flavorings, or colorings. Finally, organic food production is kinder to animals and the environment, therefore when we buy organic, we are helping to ensure that our children inherit a healthier world.

THE SOLUTION

In a world where the food industry spends millions of dollars each year promoting over-processed, fatty, sugary, and additive-laden foods to our kids, it is easy as a parent to feel powerless to change what our kids eat. The truth is no one has more influence over your child's eating habits than you, so here is how you can really make a difference.

PREPARE MORE FOOD AT HOME

The single, most effective thing you can do to improve your child's diet is to cut back on pre-prepared and processed foods and make more of it yourself at home from fresh ingredients. This may sound very time consuming but I, as a busy working mother of two, can assure you that it isn't if you follow these three simple steps:

1 Invest in some inexpensive, but essential kitchen items: plastic containers of various sizes that are freezer-, microwave-, and dishwasher-proof; airtight tins or jars for storing cakes, cookies, and bread; freezer bags of various sizes; sticky white labels for labeling frozen food.

2 Get into the habit of cooking in bulk and freezing or storing food for future use. This book is full of fast and healthy recipes made from everyday ingredients that are ideal for cooking in large quantities and freezing.

3 Establish a repertoire of four or five different healthy breakfasts, lunches, evening meals, desserts, and snacks that can be whipped up in minutes. Refer to the Real Alternatives lists at the beginning of each recipe chapter for lots of super-speedy ideas for every meal and snack of the day.

CHANGE THE WAY YOU THINK ABOUT FEEDING YOUR CHILDREN

Contrary to popular belief, children are not mini aliens beamed down from another planet that need feeding a special kid-friendly diet of fries, burgers, fish sticks, and ice cream. They don't need to be bribed and enticed into eating by brightly colored packaging, novelty toys, or gimmicks. They are mini adults and, like adults, if allowed to experience a wide variety of tastes they will eventually develop a liking for a whole range of different foods.

This applies to babies, too. Therefore it is important to educate our children's taste buds as early as possible by feeding weaning babies on a wide variety of home-cooked foods. Storebought jars may have their place occasionally, but if relied upon for every meal they will only encourage your children to develop a bland and unadventurous palette, making the future task of encouraging them to eat a varied diet of real, unprocessed foods that much harder.

Try not to insist that your children eat everything on their plate. Encourage them to start with small amounts and explain that they can always have more if they want it. Research shows that children who are taught to finish everything on their plates often lose the skill to judge for themselves when they are full and consequently can go on to become over-eaters as adults. Instead, if they insist they are full, simply remove the food but do not offer a dessert. Don't assume they won't like a food until they have tried it (unless it is very spicy).

SPRING CLEAN YOUR KITCHEN CUPBOARDS

Don't keep unhealthy foods in the house. No matter how good your intentions, if your cupboards, fridge, and freezer are filled with food and drinks that are high in fat, salt, sugar, and/or additives, they will get eaten. So clear them out and cross them off your future shopping list. Instead, take a look at Pantry Basics on pages 26–7, which includes almost everything you will need to make most of the recipes in this book and doubles as a useful shopping list.

MAKE MEALTIMES FUN

Children enjoy eating with others much more than eating alone, so try to eat with your children whenever you can. Sometimes the very act of sitting at the table together is all that is needed to encourage a child to eat more of the food on his plate.

Eating together also provides an excellent opportunity to encourage children to try new foods and to chat to them about the health benefits of the foods they are eating. Try to talk in terms that are directly relevant to them depending on their age and interests. For example, a younger child may be encouraged by the idea that certain foods will make her grow taller, run faster, or jump higher. Older children are often swayed a little more by the way a food may affect their appearance, for example the protein in homemade burgers helping muscles to grow bigger or the vitamins

WAYS TO MAKE MEALTIMES A MORE POSITIVE EXPERIENCE

Involve your children in the social aspect of sharing a meal and talk about subjects you know they are interested in.

Praise, praise, praise. Acknowledge any efforts to try a new food or to eat the foods that are served.

Put a disposal tablecloth on the table and let your kids draw on it with crayons.

Play some music.

in fresh fruit and vegetables helping to make their skin clearer and their eyes brighter.

Children also love to serve themselves. Initially, they may need a little guidance as to quantities but it is amazing how the simple act of being allowed to put their own food on their plate will entice them to eat.

LEAD BY EXAMPLE

Children learn far more from what they see and experience than from what they are told. Therefore it is vital that parents lead by example when it comes to eating and exercising.

DON'T TAKE REFUSALS TOO SERIOUSLY

Continue to present your children with a wide range of foods even if they resist them at first. If a child refuses to eat a certain food, try not to make too much of an issue of it. Simply take it away and present it again another time, possibly in a different form. For example, a child that doesn't like fresh tomatoes will often happily eat tomato soup.

ENCOURAGE A HEALTHY APPETITE

Most parents worry about their children not eating enough. However, the worst thing you can do is to offer them cookies, chips, candy, and fatty, over-processed foods in an attempt to cajole them into eating. Instead, allow them a little time to build up a healthy hunger. After all, a child that comes to the table feeling hungry is far more likely to eat a healthy balanced meal than a child that has been allowed to fill up between meals on junk. Limit snacks to a maximum of two a day (one in the morning between breakfast and lunch and one in the afternoon between lunch and dinner) and make sure the foods available to snack on are as healthy as possible.

Children have only very small stomachs and yet they have huge nutritional needs, so everything they eat should be able to justify its place. Don't have cookies, chocolate, candy, sugary drinks, and chips in the house. Instead, make sure the fruit bowl is always topped up and encourage your children to snack on

whole-wheat toast, plain yogurt, and whole-grain breakfast cereals (more healthy snack ideas can be found on page 45).

Encourage as much physical activity as possible. Children love to move and be active. Unfortunately, the opportunities for them to do

so are becoming increasingly limited. Playing outside has been replaced by watching television and time spent playing computer games is increasing. Make time in your family's daily routine for exercise, whether it's walking the dog, a bike ride, or going to the park.

LEGITIMIZE ALL FOODS

Instead of talking to your children about foods being "good" or "bad," explain to them that all foods are okay if eaten in the right amounts. If we teach this message to our children, we are a long way towards instilling healthy eating habits in them for life.

COOK TOGETHER

Encourage your children to help you cook. There may be a little more mess in the kitchen than usual, but it's a great way of teaching kids about food. Even very young children will enjoy squidging pizza dough through their fingers or cutting cookies. You'll be amazed at how much more they'll eat when they've rolled it, shaped it, or baked it themselves. By the time a child is four, he should be able to make a simple meal with a bit of help from you, and the skills he learns will stay with him for the rest of his life.

UNDERSTANDING FOOD LABELS

Although food labels are much clearer than they used to be, they can still lead to confusion, especially when it comes to understanding portion size. Check the label to make sure that what you assume is a portion size is the same as that considered to be a serving by the manufacturer. For example, you may consider a 3-oz. bag of chips to be one portion, whereas certain manufacturers consider this to be two. This means that the sodium content per portion given on the label would be for half the bag, not the whole bag.

The table below shows whether a food contains unhealthy amounts of fat, sugar, and salt. If you are looking at a food that your child is likely to eat in its entirety, like a ready meal, compare the figure per serving given on the packet with the guide. For other foods eaten in relatively small amounts, look at the nutritional information per 100 g.

UNDERSTANDING FOOD LABELS		
NUTRIENT	A LOT	A LITTLE
Total fat	20 g	3 g
Saturated fat	5 g	1 g
Sugar	10 g	3 g
Sodium	500 mg	100 mg

KEEP A CAREFUL EYE ON TELEVISION VIEWING

On average, children spend more time in front of the television than being taught at school. The number of food advertisements shown during children's programs are two to three times higher than those shown during adult viewing periods and a recent survey of these adverts found that between 95 and 99 percent of all food products advertised are high in fat, and/or salt, and/or sugar. Additional studies have also found that children who are regularly exposed to these adverts are far less able to judge the nutritional quality of foods. For these reasons, it is important to carefully monitor the amount of television your children watch.

FOOD WARNINGS

Nuts In a small number of children, nuts, especially peanuts, can cause serious allergies. Children under the age of three with a family history of allergy should not be given peanuts in any form. Children with no allergy history can be given peanuts and other nuts after the age of one. Don't give whole nuts to any child under the age of five because of the risk of choking. Always chop nuts or grind them finely.

Eggs Don't give raw eggs or food that contains raw or partially cooked eggs to young children because of the risk of salmonella, which causes food poisoning. If you give eggs to your toddler, make sure they are hard-cooked so both the white and yolk are solid.

Honey Don't give honey to children under the age of one. Occasionally, honey can contain a type of bacteria that can produce toxins in a baby's intestines causing serious illness.

YOUR KITCHEN

It can be frustrating to open a recipe book and find that your cupboards only contain half the ingredients and equipment called for. That's why I have included a list of most of the things you will need to make the recipes in this book. The list is long, but it contains lots of useful, basic items that every kitchen should have. I also hope that the information in this book about many of the commercially prepared foods you may currently have in your cupboards and freezers is enough to convince you that they can go, making room for these healthier foods.

PANTRY BASICS

RICE, GRAINS, & CEREALS
Brown rice
Basmati rice
Bulgur wheat
Oats
Wheat bran
High bran cereals
One hundred percent
   whole-grain cereals

BEANS & LEGUMES
Any canned or dried beans,
   including red kidney,
   butter, cannellini, navy,
   aduki, borlotti, pinto,
   chickpeas
Red and green split lentils

BREAD
Whole-wheat bread
Flour tortillas
Whole-wheat pita
   bread
Rye bread

PASTA & NOODLES
Whole-wheat pasta—different
   shapes and sizes such as
   penne, spaghetti, farfalle
Whole-wheat couscous
Noodles (any sort)

NUTS & SEEDS
Brazil nuts
Cashew nuts

Flaked almonds
Hazelnuts
Pecan nuts
Unsalted peanuts
Walnuts
Flaxseed
Poppy seeds
Pumpkin seeds
Sesame seeds
Sunflower seeds

DAIRY & EGGS
Eggs
Milk
Sour cream
Fromage frais
Plain yogurt

Cottage cheese
Low-fat Cheddar cheese
Soft cheeses

MEAT, POULTRY, & FISH
Prosciutto and bacon
Lean ground beef
Extra lean ham and turkey
   slices (fresh from the deli
   counter, not processed)
Chicken breast (skin removed)
Mackerel
Sardines (canned and fresh)
Smoked salmon
Wild or organic salmon
   fillets
Cod (frozen or fresh)

Haddock (frozen or fresh)

Tuna (canned in spring water
and fresh)

FRUIT

Any, particularly apples, pears,
plums, cherries, peaches,
strawberries, raspberries,
blackberries, kiwi fruit,
oranges, limes, lemons,
grapefruit, red grapes

Canned fruit in fruit juice rather
than syrup

Frozen mixed berries

Dried fruit including apricots,
dates, figs, and raisins

VEGETABLES

As many different colored fresh
vegetables as possible

Potatoes and sweet potatoes

Frozen vegetables—these can be
just as nutritious as fresh
ones and meals can be made
from them in no time

HERBS & FLAVORINGS

A choice of fresh cilantro, basil,
oregano, rosemary, parsley,
sage, and mint

Garlic

Ginger

Mild curry powder

Ground cumin

BAKING

Whole-wheat flour

Oatmeal

Baking powder

Apple pie spice

Ground ginger

Ground cinnamon

FATS & OILS

Virgin olive oil, for cooking

Sunflower oil, for cooking and
baking

Extra virgin cold pressed olive
oil for use in salad dressings

Polyunsaturated spread or
sunflower margarine

Unsalted butter

STAPLES

Organic vegetable broth

Soy sauce

Worcestershire sauce

Tomato paste

Olives

Balsamic vinegar

Red wine vinegar

Good quality semisweet
chocolate with 70 percent
cocoa solids

All-natural peanut butter

Honey

Canned tomatoes

Cornstarch

DRINKS

Unsweetened fresh fruit and
vegetable juices, preferably
with pulp

Sparkling mineral water

ESSENTIAL EQUIPMENT

You will probably have most of this equipment in your kitchen
already. When it comes to essential items, buy the best you
can afford so that they will last.

Freezer

Freezerproof and
microwaveable plastic
food containers in
various sizes

Plastic wrap, parchment
paper, and aluminum foil

Plastic food bags

Sticky labels

Food processor

Blender

Weighing scales—electronic
scales are easy for
children to use

Lightweight plastic or
metal bowls

Measuring jug

Set of cup measures

Rolling pin

Assorted cookie cutters

3 saucepans—small,
medium, and large

Steamer

Nonstick skillet

Nonstick wok with lid

Stovetop grill pan

2 baking trays

Nonstick roasting pan

Assorted cake and
bread pans

Wire cooling rack

Paper muffin pan liners

Large chopping board

Set of sharp knives

Garlic crusher

Can opener

Potato masher

Box grater

Colander

Strainer

2 wooden spoons

2 tablespoons

2 teaspoons

Slotted metal spoon

Plastic spatula

A solid chair or stool for
your child to stand on to
reach work surface height

6 ramekins—⅔ cup each

Ovenproof dish

OPTIONAL EQUIPMENT

Microwave

Yogurt maker

Ice cream maker

Bread maker

Mortar and pestle

Mini blender for making
pesto and grinding nuts
and seeds

RECIPES

BREAKFAST

A GOOD START TO THE DAY

Breakfast is arguably the most important meal of the day, especially for children. Even when we are asleep our bodies continue to burn calories. Children generally sleep for long periods, so by the time they wake up their blood sugar levels are naturally depleted. As breakfast provides a major part of a child's daily energy supply, if breakfast is skipped it can result in lethargy, mood swings, food cravings, excessive hunger, and an impaired ability to think and learn. Research shows that kids who eat breakfast are less inclined to crave fatty, sugary foods and are more likely to meet their daily requirements of certain essential vitamins and minerals than those who skip it.

GETTING IT RIGHT

The nutritional quality of commercially prepared breakfast cereals varies wildly from one packet to the next. Some offer a highly nutritious, vitamin-, mineral-, and fiber-packed start to your child's day, while the majority are little more than highly processed junk full of fat, sugar, and salt. A recent survey of 28 breakfast cereals marketed specifically at children found nearly one-third of them contained 40 percent sugar and 64 percent had excessive amounts of salt.

Many of the sugary, processed cereals targeted at children have been so highly refined that they are not only stripped of most of their natural goodness, they are also broken down by the body very quickly when eaten. This causes blood sugar levels to surge and then plummet, which in turn can result in behavioral problems and hyperactivity followed by tiredness, tantrums, and an inability to concentrate.

The best way to avoid this roller coaster effect on blood sugar levels is to encourage kids to eat foods that release their sugars more slowly into the blood stream, such as whole-wheat cereals, oats, fruit, and whole-wheat bread. Breakfast consisting of these foods will ensure your child has a steady supply of energy to draw on throughout the morning.

CEREALS
REAL ALTERNATIVES

bran flakes soaked in milk, served with a spoonful of yogurt and some fresh raspberries • oatmeal • 100 percent whole-grain shredded wheat biscuits sprinkled with chopped dried apricots • whole-wheat biscuits with warm milk, sliced banana, and raisins

EGGS AND TOAST
REAL ALTERNATIVES

hard-cooked eggs mashed with some chopped organic ham and spread on a slice of whole-wheat toast • whole-grain English muffin, toasted and lightly buttered or spread with tahini paste and honey

FRUIT AND YOGURT
REAL ALTERNATIVES

plain yogurt flavored with fruit compote, fresh fruit, dried apricots, honey, or finely chopped nuts and seeds • hot fruit kabobs with honey, a sprinkling of sesame seeds, and yogurt • a halved kiwi fruit served with a teaspoon and some hot buttered whole-wheat toast • warm fruit compote (page 121), blended with a ripe banana and mixed with a dollop of sour cream • 1 chopped apple and 1 pear mixed with raisins, heated in a microwave until soft, then mixed with yogurt and cinnamon

AVOID	REPLACE WITH
Cereals marketed specifically at kids, especially those described as "frosted," and chocolate cereals	Products labeled "whole-wheat" or "whole bran," porridge oats, or homemade Muesli (page 32)
Commercially prepared breakfast bars	Homemade alternatives (page 32)
White bread	Whole-grain, nutty, or stone-ground varieties
Sweetened yogurts and those marketed specifically at kids	Plain or Greek yogurt or fromage frais flavored with honey, natural fruit puree, or fresh fruit
Flavored milks and commercial milk shakes	Plain milk, homemade smoothies, and milk shakes

BREAKFAST BARS

These bars make a great snack at any time of the day or include them in packed lunches.

PREPARATION TIME 12–15 minutes
COOKING TIME 15–20 minutes

1¼ cups old-fashioned rolled oats

¼ cup raisins

⅓ cup dried apricots, finely chopped

¼ cup dried papaya, finely chopped

¼ cup stoned dates, finely chopped

2 tablespoons slivered almonds

2 tablespoons sesame seeds

2 tablespoons honey

3 tablespoons smooth peanut butter

1 egg white

a baking pan, 8 × 10 inches, lightly oiled and lined with nonstick parchment paper

makes 14 bars

Put the oats in a large bowl. Add all the dried fruit, nuts, and seeds and mix well.

Put the honey and peanut butter in a small saucepan and heat gently, stirring occasionally with a wooden spoon until smooth. Pour into the oat mixture and mix well.

Put the egg white in a small bowl and beat with a small wire whisk until light and frothy. Add it to the oat mixture and mix with a wooden spoon until the mixture sticks together. Spoon the mixture into the prepared pan, then press it down with the back of the spoon, making the surface as even as possible.

Bake in a preheated oven at 375°F for 15–20 minutes until the top is golden and feels firm to the touch. Remove from the oven and let cool slightly in the pan before cutting into 14 bars. Let cool completely before removing them from the pan. Store the bars in an airtight container for up to 5 days.

MUESLI

Breakfasts don't come more nutrient-packed than this. The nuts and seeds are full of vitamins, minerals, and essential fatty acids. The oats and wheat germ will stabilize blood sugars and provide a constant source of energy throughout the morning. and the dried fruit is a fabulous source of fiber helping to keep all the digestive processes working properly. Add to that the calcium-rich milk or yogurt and sliced fresh fruit—you couldn't give your family a better start to the day.

PREPARATION TIME 10 minutes
COOKING TIME 10–15 minutes

¼ cup sunflower seeds

¼ cup pumpkin seeds

2 tablespoons flaxseed

⅓ cup slivered almonds

⅓ cup hazelnuts, chopped

3 cups old-fashioned rolled oats

¼ cup wheat germ

¼ cup dried apricots, chopped

¼ cup dried banana

¼ cup golden raisins

¼ cup dried cherries or cranberries

to serve
1 banana, sliced, or a small handful of fresh berries or seedless grapes

cold milk or plain yogurt

2 baking trays
makes about 2 lb.

Sprinkle all the seeds and nuts on one baking tray and the oats on another. Cook in a preheated oven at 400°F for 10–12 minutes or until lightly toasted. Remove from the oven and let cool.

Once cool, put the nuts, seeds, and oats in a large airtight container. Add the wheat germ and all the dried fruit, then either stir to mix or close the lid securely and shake well. Store in a cool dry cupboard until required.

To serve, spoon about 5 tablespoons muesli into a cereal bowl, top with fresh fruit, and pour over some milk or add some yogurt.

COOK'S TIP

- This is a recipe which children can help to make. Don't worry about being too exact with the measurements.

VARIATIONS

- Serve this as a dry snack, without the milk or yogurt, in small paper bags instead of salted peanuts or potato chips.
- Use as a topping to add crunch to yogurts.
- **Granola** Put all the muesli ingredients in a large bowl and add 2 tablespoons maple syrup. Mix well. Transfer to 1 or 2 nonstick baking trays and bake in a preheated oven at 325°F for about 40 minutes, stirring halfway through, until crisp and golden. Serve with cold milk.

PINK PORRIDGE

Oats are an excellent source of slow-releasing sugars as well as fiber, iron, zinc, and B vitamins. By adding some fresh fruit, you are making an already excellent breakfast even more nutritious and adding novelty value at the same time!

PREPARATION TIME 5 minutes

COOKING TIME 4–5 minutes, plus 2 minutes standing time

½ cup old-fashioned rolled oats

2 tablespoons wheat bran

2½ cups milk (see cook's tips)

½ cup strawberries, hulled, or raspberries, plus extra for serving

1–2 teaspoons honey (optional)

serves 2–4

Put the oats, bran, and milk in a large microwaveable bowl and cover with microwaveable wrap. Pierce the wrap and heat in a microwave on HIGH for 4–5 minutes. Stir and let stand for 2 minutes.

Transfer the porridge to a blender, add the fruit, and process until smooth. Add honey, if using, to taste. If necessary, return the porridge to the microwaveable bowl and reheat on HIGH for 1 minute.

To serve, spoon into individual bowls and top with a few whole strawberries or raspberries.

COOK'S TIPS

- Use whole milk for children under the age of 5, low-fat milk for children over 5.
- To make the porridge on the hob, pour the milk into a nonstick saucepan and sprinkle in the oats and wheat bran. Heat gently, stirring occasionally, for 2–3 minutes until thickened. Let cool slightly, then add the fruit and honey. Transfer to a blender and process until smooth.

VARIATION

- Replace the strawberries or raspberries with 1 sliced banana and ½ teaspoon ground cinnamon.

OVERNIGHT OATS

This is very simple to make. It can be whipped up in minutes and provides an excellent alternative to many of the sugar- and salt-laden commercially prepared breakfast cereals.

PREPARATION TIME 10 minutes

COOKING TIME 3–4 minutes

base mixture

1½ cups old-fashioned rolled oats

¼ cup wheat bran

¼ cup flaxseed

¼ cup sunflower seeds

¼ cup golden raisins

2 tablespoons finely chopped mixed nuts

to serve, per ¼ cup serving

1¼ cups low-fat milk
(use whole milk for children under 5)

½ apple, peeled, cored and grated

1 tablespoon plain yogurt

fresh fruit, such as apricots and berries

makes about 2½ cups; serves 8

Put all the ingredients for the base mixture in an airtight container and close securely. Shake well to mix, then store in a cool cupboard until required.

The night before you want to serve the oats, put ¼ cup of the mixture in a bowl and cover with ¾ cup milk. Stir in the grated apple, cover the bowl with plastic wrap, and leave in the refrigerator overnight.

The following morning, add a little more milk to the bowl to slacken the mixture. Transfer the mixture to a nonstick saucepan and heat gently, stirring, until hot, 3–4 minutes. Alternatively, put the mixture in a microwaveable bowl and heat in a microwave on HIGH for 2 minutes. Stir, then let stand for 1 minute.

To serve, top with the yogurt and some fresh fruit.

COOK'S TIP

- If you prefer a nutty, crisp texture, omit the nuts from the base mix and sprinkle them on top, to serve.

APPLE & OAT MUFFINS

These muffins are made with sunflower oil and yogurt, so they are moist without having the high saturated fat content of most commercially prepared versions. Serve them warm on a cold morning or eat them as a snack at any time of the day. They also make a delicious dessert, served with some Homemade Custard (page 126) or warm fruit compote (page 121) and a dollop of reduced fat sour cream or crème fraîche.

PREPARATION TIME 5 minutes
COOKING TIME 15–18 minutes

¾ cup whole-wheat flour

¾ cup white self-rising flour

2 teaspoons baking powder

1 teaspoon baking soda

1 teaspoon apple pie spice

2 tablespoons wheat bran

¼ cup light brown sugar

¼ cup golden raisins

2 apples, about 8 oz., cored and finely chopped

2 tablespoons pecans, chopped

¼ cup dates, chopped

½ cup sunflower oil

2 eggs, beaten

2 tablespoons plain yogurt

1 tablespoon sesame seeds

a 12-hole muffin pan, lined with 12 paper muffin liners

makes 12

Sift the flours, baking powder, baking soda, and apple pie spice into a large bowl. Add any bran left in the sifter and the wheat bran and mix.

Add the sugar, raisins, apples, pecans, and dates and mix lightly with a wooden spoon. Make a well in the center, add the oil and eggs, and stir to mix. Add the yogurt and stir lightly, until just mixed (do not overmix or the muffins will be dry).

Spoon the mixture into the muffin cups until three-quarters full. Sprinkle the sesame seeds over the top, then bake in a preheated oven at 400°F for 15–18 minutes until firm to the touch. Remove from the oven and let cool slightly. Serve warm. The muffins can be wrapped and frozen for up to 1 month.

COOK'S TIP
• Bake ahead of time, then reheat in a microwave on HIGH for 20–25 seconds.

VARIATIONS
• Replace the apples with 2 ripe mashed bananas and use extra chopped pitted dates in place of the golden raisins.
• Replace the golden raisins with chopped dried fruit, such as apricots, papaya, or mango and use shredded coconut in place of the pecans. Sprinkle slivered almonds over the top before baking.
• Use ground ginger, ground cinnamon, or finely grated orange or lemon zest in place of the apple pie spice.

Did You Know?
Apples and oats are two excellent foods to eat for breakfast because they both have a very low rating on the glycemic index. This means that after being eaten they release their sugars very slowly into the blood stream, which helps to keep energy levels constant all morning and hunger pangs at bay.

EASY WHOLE-WHEAT BREAD

Many of the breads available today have been so highly refined that even the whole-wheat varieties release their sugars far too quickly into the blood stream. Many also contain preservatives to increase their shelf life, salt to add taste, and colorings to make them look more appealing. Homemade bread on the other hand is free from all those unnecessary additives, is great fun to make, and not as difficult as you might think.

PREPARATION TIME
25 minutes, plus 1 hour proving time
COOKING TIME 40–45 minutes

6 cups stone-ground whole-wheat bread flour

3 cups strong white bread flour, plus extra for sprinkling and dusting

2 sachets (2 tablespoons) quick-acting yeast

1 tablespoon sea salt

2 tablespoons light brown sugar

½ cup flaxseed

6 tablespoons olive oil

4 cups warm water

1 tablespoon poppy, sesame, or sunflower seeds

2 large baking trays, greased, or 2 loaf pans, 9 x 3 inches each, greased

makes 2 large loaves

Sift the flours into a large bowl, adding the bran left in the sifter. Stir in the yeast, salt, sugar, and flaxseed. Make a well in the flour and pour in the olive oil and the warm water. Gradually mix the flour into the liquid with your hands until the mixture comes together to make a ball.

Turn the dough out onto a lightly floured counter and knead thoroughly for 10 minutes until the dough feels smooth and very elastic. Divide the dough in half. Gently shape the dough into 2 neat balls and set the loaves on the prepared baking trays. Alternatively, they can be shaped into 2 cylinders and put in the loaf pans. Put the trays or pans in large, lightly oiled plastic bags and leave in a warm place out of any drafts for at least 1 hour or until the loaves have doubled in size.

Uncover the loaves, brush the tops with a little water, and sprinkle with the seeds of your choice. Bake in a preheated oven at 450°F for 15 minutes, then reduce the heat to 400°F and bake for another 25 to 30 minutes until golden brown. To test if the loaves are cooked, turn them upside down and tap your knuckles on the base of the loaf. It should sound hollow.

Remove the loaves from the oven, transfer to a wire rack, and let cool completely before cutting. Homemade bread is best eaten on the day it's made. Once completely cold, wrap the loaves and store them in an earthenware or wooden bread box.

COOK'S TIPS

- For crusty loaves, leave them to cool uncovered; for a soft crust, cover with a dry dish towel, then let cool.
- The loaves can be frozen for up to 1 month. Let thaw thoroughly and warm through, if desired, before serving.

VARIATIONS

- Add ¼ cup sunflower seeds and 2 tablespoons sesame seeds to the basic bread mix.
- Add ¾ cup chopped walnuts and ½ cup finely chopped pitted dates to the basic bread mix.
- Add 1¼ cups finely chopped mixed dried fruit, such as golden raisins and apricots, to the basic bread mix.
- Add ¼ cup freshly chopped herbs to the basic bread mix. Try rosemary, parsley, and thyme, or sage, thyme, and chives, or use a herb-flavored olive oil.
- Instead of the olive oil, use walnut oil and add 1½ cups finely chopped walnuts to the basic bread mix.
- For a richer loaf, replace some of the whole-wheat flour with spelt, add a beaten egg to the basic bread mix, and use milk instead of the water.
- Shape the dough into small round rolls and bake for 10–15 minutes.
- Make bread sticks to use as dippers (page 48).

Did You Know?

Whole-wheat flour has twice as much potassium, nearly three times more fiber, and six times more magnesium than white flour.

EGGS

Eggs are nature's "fast food." One egg can provide up to 20 percent of a child's daily protein requirement. They also contain potassium, iodine, folic acid, beta-carotene, and iron. They can be whipped up in minutes to provide many different nutritious meals. Buy organic eggs whenever possible, because not only are they naturally richer in omega 3 fatty acids, they come from chickens that have been fed on a natural diet, free from the large amounts of growth-promoting antibiotics routinely fed to non-organic chickens.

DIPPY EGGS

To prevent eggs from cracking when put in boiling water, make sure they are at room temperature before cooking.

Put an egg on a tablespoon and carefully lower it into a saucepan three-quarters full of gently simmering water. For soft-boiled eggs, cook for 4 minutes. Remove the egg from the water with a large slotted spoon, place it in an egg cup, and tap firmly on the shell to crack it and stop the egg from cooking further.

If you prefer hard-cooked eggs, cook for 10 minutes in boiling water.

Serve with fingers of whole-wheat toast.

COOK'S TIP
• Don't give soft-boiled eggs to young children. Make sure both the white and yolk are solid.

PREPARATION TIME 5 minutes
COOKING TIME 8 minutes

2 eggs

1 tablespoon water or milk

2 teaspoons virgin olive oil

¼ cup chopped lean ham

sea salt and freshly ground black pepper

an omelet pan or small skillet, 6 inches diameter

serves 1–2

HAM OMELET

Break the eggs into a bowl, add the water or milk, and salt and pepper to taste. Whisk briefly with a fork or a wire whisk.

Heat the oil in the omelet pan or skillet and swirl it around to coat the bottom of the pan. Pour in the egg mixture, then use a fork to pull the set egg mixture that forms at the edges of the pan into the center, letting the uncooked egg flow back to the edges. When lightly set, sprinkle in the ham and cook for another 2 minutes. Fold the omelet over and slide it onto a warmed plate. Serve immediately.

VARIATIONS
• Add 1 chopped tomato with the ham.
• Add 2 tablespoons grated reduced-fat Cheddar cheese when you add the ham.
• Add 1 tablespoon chopped fresh mixed herbs to the eggs before pouring them into the pan.

POACHED EGGS

Half fill a skillet with water and bring to a boil. Reduce to a gentle simmer, then add a little lemon juice or vinegar to the water. Break an egg into a cup then pour it carefully into the pan.

Alternatively, put some lightly oiled round cookie cutters in the water and slip the eggs into these. Cook for 4 to 5 minutes or until cooked to your liking. Remove with a slotted spoon and serve immediately.

SCRAMBLED EGGS

Beat 1 egg with 1 tablespoon milk and a little black pepper, to taste. Melt a small knob of polyunsaturated spread in a small saucepan or heat 1 teaspoon virgin olive oil until hot. Pour in the beaten egg and cook, stirring continuously, for 2 to 3 minutes until set and creamy.

Alternatively, put the egg mixture in a microwaveable bowl and heat in a microwave on HIGH for 2 minutes, stirring halfway through.

Serve on top of whole-wheat toast.

SMOOTHIES

Smoothies can be a great way of encouraging otherwise reluctant children to eat breakfast. They are also a fabulous way of increasing the amount of fruit your child eats. Here are a few ideas to start you off, but let your children experiment with a whole range of fruit and other ingredients until they find one that they really like.

SUMMER BERRY BREAKFAST

PREPARATION TIME 5 minutes

¾ cup fresh berries, such as strawberries or raspberries

⅔ cup plain yogurt

1¼ cups low-fat milk, chilled (use whole milk for children under 5)

2 tablespoons crushed ice, to serve (optional)

serves 2

Put the berries, yogurt, and milk in a blender and process for 1 minute until smooth. Put 1 tablespoon crushed ice, if using, in each of 2 tall glasses, then pour the smoothie over the top. Decorate the edge of the glasses with a couple of berries, if desired.

COOK'S TIP
• Frozen summer berries, defrosted, will work just as well and are as nutritious as fresh.

FULL OF FRUIT SMOOTHIE

PREPARATION TIME 10 minutes

1 small ripe mango, peeled, pit removed, and flesh cut into small pieces

1 small ripe papaya, cut in half, seeded, and flesh cut into small pieces

2 nectarines, cut in half and pits removed

4 slices fresh pineapple, peeled and cut into small pieces

½ cup freshly squeezed orange juice

2 tablespoons wheat bran

about 3 tablespoons crushed ice

serves 2

Put the fruit, orange juice, and wheat bran in a blender and process to form a puree. Add 1 tablespoon crushed ice and blend again. Put 1 tablespoon crushed ice in each of 2 tall glasses, pour the smoothie over, and serve.

GET UP 'N' GO SMOOTHIE

PREPARATION TIME 5–7 minutes

2 medium bananas, sliced

3 tablespoons smooth peanut butter

⅔ cup plain yogurt

1¼ cups low-fat milk, chilled (use whole milk for children under 5)

2 tablespoons crushed ice, to serve

serves 2

Put the bananas, peanut butter, and yogurt in a blender and process for about 1 minute until smooth.

Add the milk and process again until smooth. Put 1 tablespoon crushed ice in each of 2 tall glasses, pour the smoothie over, and serve.

SESAME STREET

PREPARATION TIME 6–8 minutes

2 ripe melon wedges, about 3 oz., seeds and skin removed and flesh chopped

¾ cup fresh or frozen raspberries, defrosted

2 medium bananas

1 tablespoon sesame seeds

1 tablespoon tahini (ground sesame seed paste)

1¼ cups low-fat milk, chilled (use whole milk for children under 5)

1–2 teaspoons honey

serves 2

Put all the fruit in a blender and process to form a puree. Add 2 teaspoons sesame seeds and the tahini paste and process for 1 minute. With the motor running, gradually pour in the milk and honey and process until smooth. Pour the smoothie into 2 tall glasses, sprinkle with the remaining sesame seeds, and serve.

LUNCH BOXES, SNACKS, & DRINKS

LUNCH BOXES

Preparing children's lunch boxes can be a laborious task for busy parents. With little time to think about new variations, we tend to revert to the tried and tested formula of a sandwich, often with a high fat filling, chips, a storebought cookie, a "fruit" yogurt, a carton of juice, and the obligatory apple. Not only does this get repetitive for our kids, it also amounts to a lot of fat and sugar. In fact, a lunch such as this can contain more than 45 g of fat—approximately 80 percent of the fat a child should eat in a day—and almost 11 teaspoons of sugar, more than a child's daily recommended amount.

SNACKS

Snacking on healthy foods between meals can be a great way of topping up energy levels. However, most commercially prepared snacks are extremely high in fat, salt, sugar, and additives and sadly lacking in any real nutritional value. The more of these snacks children eat, the higher their intake of fat, salt, sugar, and additives becomes and the less room there is for healthier foods like fruit and vegetables, resulting in serious short- and long-term health problems.

Savory snacks are commonly seen as a healthier alternative to candy because they appear to contain less sugar and are made from foods we perceive to be healthy, such as corn. In reality, they are often high in fat, especially saturated fat, and many contain artificial sweeteners and often very high levels of salt.

A recent survey that looked at the nutritional content of 283 commercially prepared snack foods found:

- The average snack had over 5 additives
- One-third contained colorings and 70 percent contained flavorings or flavor enhancers
- One-fifth had high levels of hydrogenated fat
- One-quarter contained more than 30 percent sugar; some had as much as 57 percent
- Poor labeling and misleading health claims on packaging made it hard to make healthy choices
- Fifty-five percent of chips and snacks contained over twice the recommended level of saturated fat
- Potato chips and savory snacks had the highest levels in salt, with some 2 oz. portions providing over half the salt a child should eat in a day

DRINKS

Kids need to drink one to two quarts of fluids a day to keep them fully hydrated. Insufficient fluids can result in headaches, reduced coordination, tiredness, a loss of stamina, and an inability to concentrate. However, drinking healthily is as important as eating well.

Kids consume 30 times more soft drinks today than they did 50 years ago. Most fruit drinks contain very little fruit juice: they are mainly water and sugar (or artificial sweeteners) and are full of additives. Sodas have very few, if any, nutrients and a can of cola can contain up to 7 teaspoons of sugar, almost the maximum daily amount for a six-year-old.

**SAVORY SNACKS
REAL ALTERNATIVES**
mixed, unsalted nuts and raisins • green beans wrapped in prosciutto • celery filled with herby cream cheese • olives • sliced ham spread with hummus and wrapped around carrot sticks • Cheddar cheese squares topped with grapes

**SWEET SNACKS
REAL ALTERNATIVES**
chopped fresh fruit with nuts, seeds, and raisins • dry, homemade Muesli (page 32) and raisins • plain yogurt with honey or fruit compote (page 121) • a whole fruit, such as a nectarine or plum • Chocolate-dipped Fruit (page 139)

**DRINKS REAL
ALTERNATIVES**
add a small amount of fresh fruit juice, crushed ice, mint leaves, or lemon slices to uncarbonated spring water • add a little fruit-flavored syrup to sparkling mineral water • freshly squeezed vegetable and fruit juices • homemade milk shakes (page 71) and smoothies (page 42) • warm milk and honey

HONEY ROASTED NUTS & SEEDS

Nuts and seeds are full of protein, vitamins, minerals, and essential fatty acids. This snack has all this goodness without the high levels of saturated fat and salt of the storebought varieties.

PREPARATION TIME 3 minutes
COOKING TIME 10–15 minutes

16 oz. assorted whole skinned nuts, such as cashews, hazelnuts, and almonds

8 oz. assorted seeds, such as sunflower and pumpkin

2 tablespoons honey

1 tablespoon organic soy sauce

serves 8–10

Put the nuts and seeds in a roasting pan in an even layer. Cook in a preheated oven at 400°F for 10 to 15 minutes, stirring occasionally, until golden brown.

Put the honey and soy sauce in a bowl and mix well. As soon as the nuts are removed from the oven, pour the honey mixture over them and stir until thoroughly coated. Let cool completely before serving. Store in an airtight container for up to 1 week.

COOK'S TIP

- If you want to store the nuts and seeds for longer, roast them as in the main recipe, then let cool and store. To coat them, reheat the nuts for 5 minutes in a dry skillet, stirring frequently, then pour over the honey mixture, and stir until coated.

VEGETABLE CHIPS

These are a great way to increase your child's vegetable intake. However, they are fairly high in fat, so go easy.

PREPARATION TIME
25–30 minutes
COOKING TIME 30 minutes

1 beet

1 sweet potato

1 parsnip

1 large carrot

sunflower oil, for frying

serves 8–10

Peel all the vegetables. Using a vegetable peeler, preferably a swivel bladed one, peel very thin slices from the vegetables. Put some oil in a large saucepan or wok to a depth of 4 inches. Alternatively, fill a deep-fryer to the manufacturer's recommended level. Heat the oil to 325°F. Add batches of the thinly sliced vegetables to the hot oil (use a frying basket, if you have one) and blanch them for 1 minute until soft but not crisp. Remove the vegetable slices and drain on paper towels. Repeat with the remaining vegetable slices.

Increase the temperature of the oil to 350°F and fry a batch of the softened vegetable slices for about 1 minute until crisp. Remove and drain on paper towels. Repeat with the remaining vegetable slices. Let cool, then serve. Once cold, the chips can be stored in an airtight container for up to 24 hours.

DIPS

Kids love dunking a stick of carrot or a chunk of bread into dips. Storebought dips can be okay, but read the label carefully to check that they aren't full of additives or overloaded with saturated fat and salt. These homemade dips are incredibly easy to make, packed with flavor and nutrients, and great for quick suppers, packed lunches, or parties.

CREAMY GARLIC DIP

Garlic contains allicin, which has been shown to be particularly effective at strengthening the immune system, especially when eaten raw.

PREPARATION TIME 5 minutes

⅔ cup sour cream

1–2 garlic cloves, crushed

1 tablespoon chopped fresh cilantro

freshly ground black pepper

to serve

Vegetable Sticks (see below)

Bread Sticks (see below)

serves 4; makes ⅔ cup

Put the sour cream, garlic, cilantro, and pepper, to taste, in a small bowl and mix well. Serve with vegetable or bread sticks for dipping.

If not using immediately, cover tightly with plastic wrap and store for up to 2 days in the refrigerator.

VARIATION

• Add 1 teaspoon curry paste or powder to the dip. Let stand for 30 minutes so the curry flavor can develop.

CRUNCHY DIP

Children that can weigh, measure, and use a food processor will love making this dip. It's high in protein, calcium, and omega 3 fatty acids.

PREPARATION TIME
5–8 minutes, plus cooling time
COOKING TIME
10–12 minutes

¾ cup sesame seeds

1 teaspoon coriander seeds

¾ cup skinned hazelnuts

1 teaspoon ground cumin

to serve

Vegetable Sticks (see right)

Creamy Garlic Dip (see above)

2 baking trays

serves 8; makes 1 cup

Put the seeds on one baking tray and the hazelnuts on another. Cook the seeds in a preheated oven at 350°F for 8 to 10 minutes until they begin to smell fragrant and look toasted. Cook the hazelnuts at the same temperature for 10 to 12 minutes or until golden brown.

Let cool slightly, then transfer the seeds and nuts to a food processor, using a funnel if necessary. Blend until finely crushed (don't blend for too long or they will turn to a paste). Stir in the ground cumin.

To serve, dip vegetable sticks into the Creamy Garlic Dip (or any of the dips on page 51), then into the toasted nuts and seeds. Store the crunchy dip in an airtight container in the refrigerator for up to 3 days.

DIPPERS

VEGETABLE STICKS

• Take any firm raw vegetables, such as bell peppers, carrots, cucumber, zucchini, and celery. Wash thoroughly, peel if necessary, then cut into matchsticks.
• Divide broccoli or cauliflower into tiny florets.
• Cut cherry tomatoes in half.
• Use trimmed sugarsnap peas.

BREAD STICKS

• Make 1 quantity Easy Whole-wheat Bread dough (page 38). Divide the dough into small pieces, about the size of an apricot, then roll them in your hands to form thin sticks, about 4 inches long and 1 inch wide. Put them on a greased baking tray and bake in a preheated oven at 450°F for 8 to 10 minutes until lightly golden and crispy. Alternatively, toast a whole-wheat pita bread and slice it into fingers for dipping.

GUACAMOLE

Avocados have the highest protein content of any fruit and are rich in mono-unsaturated fat (the type of fat that is linked with lowering the risk of heart disease, cancer, and obesity). They are also a good source of vitamin C.

PREPARATION TIME
5–8 minutes

2 ripe avocados, peeled and pits removed

2 tablespoons freshly squeezed lemon or lime juice

2 ripe tomatoes

1 garlic clove, crushed

freshly ground black pepper

to serve

Vegetable Sticks (page 48)

Bread Sticks (page 48)

serves 4–6

Chop the avocados into small pieces and put them in a small bowl. Add the lemon or lime juice and toss well.

Cut the tomatoes into quarters and remove and discard the seeds, if you like. Put the tomatoes, garlic, avocado pieces, and black pepper, to taste, in a food processor. Blend for 1 to 2 minutes until smooth. Transfer to a small serving bowl and serve with vegetable sticks and bread sticks for dipping.

If not using immediately, cover the bowl tightly with plastic wrap and store in the refrigerator for up to 24 hours.

COOK'S TIP

- When choosing avocados to use immediately, select ones that are soft when touched but not squashy or badly discolored on their skins. If buying a few days in advance, choose fruit that are firm and free from blemishes. Store at room temperature—they can discolor if stored in the refrigerator.

HUMMUS

This dip contains lots of calcium and protein from the chickpeas and tahini, as well as iron, magnesium, and fiber. It also has the immune-boosting power of garlic.

PREPARATION TIME 5–8 minutes

14 oz. canned chickpeas, rinsed and drained

2 tablespoons tahini (ground sesame seed paste)

2 tablespoons freshly squeezed lemon juice

2–3 tablespoons olive oil

1 garlic clove, crushed

to serve

Vegetable Sticks (page 48)

Bread Sticks (page 48)

serves 6–8

Put all the ingredients in a food processor and blend, using the pulse button, to form a smooth puree, about 1 minute. If the mixture is too stiff, add another tablespoon of oil and a little cooled boiled water. Serve with vegetable sticks or bread sticks for dipping.

The dip can be covered with plastic wrap and stored in the refrigerator for up to 3 days.

ROASTED ROOT DIPPERS

This is another great way to encourage your children to eat more vegetables.

PREPARATION TIME 10 minutes
COOKING TIME 40–50 minutes

1 sweet potato

1 parsnip

1 carrot

1 potato

2 tablespoons olive oil

a selection of dips, to serve

serves 4–6

Peel the vegetables and cut them into thick, chunky chips. Put them in a roasting pan, pour over the oil, and toss well to coat.

Roast in a preheated oven at 375°F for 40 to 50 minutes, stirring occasionally, until the vegetables are tender. Serve immediately with dips of your choice.

SMOKED TROUT PÂTÉ

Trout is an oily fish and is therefore a great source of omega 3 fatty acids, which promote healthy brain development and help reduce the risk of heart disease in later life.

PREPARATION TIME
12–15 minutes

5 oz. smoked trout fillets

3½ oz. cream cheese

1–2 tablespoons freshly squeezed lemon juice

1 tablespoon chopped fresh dill

freshly ground black pepper

to serve

dill sprigs

whole-wheat pita bread, toasted

serves 4–6

Remove any fine bones from the trout fillets, then break them up into tiny pieces.

Put the cream cheese and 1 tablespoon lemon juice in a small bowl and beat with a wooden spoon until soft and creamy. Stir in the trout, dill, and pepper, to taste. Add more lemon juice, if necessary, to give a spreading consistency. Cover with plastic wrap and chill in the refrigerator for 30 minutes.

To serve, sprinkle with dill sprigs and accompany with toasted whole-wheat pita bread.

Store, covered, in the refrigerator for up to 2 days.

Did You Know?

A diet rich in omega 3 and omega 6 fatty acids—found in oily fish, nuts, and seeds—may improve the behavioral patterns of children with attention deficit disorder.

VEGETABLE & NUT PÂTÉ

Nuts and seeds are full of protein and brain-boosting, immune-strengthening essential fatty acids. This recipe combines them with carrots, celery, and leeks to make a really nutritious pâté.

PREPARATION TIME 12–15 minutes
COOKING TIME 15 minutes

1 celery stalk, finely chopped

1 small carrot, finely chopped

1 small leek, finely chopped

1 small onion, finely chopped

¼ cup sunflower seeds

⅓ cup hazelnuts

5 medium mushrooms, chopped

1 garlic clove, crushed

1 teaspoon organic vegetable bouillon powder made up to ¼ cup stock

freshly ground black pepper

Vegetable Sticks or Bread Sticks (page 48), to serve

serves 6–8

Put the celery, carrot, leek, and onion in a steamer over a pan of gently simmering water and steam for 15 minutes until soft. Remove from the heat and let cool slightly.

Meanwhile, put the sunflower seeds and hazelnuts in a food processor and blend until finely ground. Remove and set aside.

Transfer the vegetables to the food processor, add the mushrooms and garlic, and using the pulse button, blend until a puree is formed.

Add the ground sunflower seeds and hazelnuts, bouillon, and black pepper, and blend again until thoroughly mixed. Spoon into a small bowl, cover, and chill in the refrigerator for 30 minutes.

Serve with vegetable sticks or bread sticks.

SMOKED SALMON & CREAM CHEESE BAGEL

PREPARATION TIME 10–12 minutes

4 sesame seed bagels, cut in half

2–3 tablespoons low-fat cream cheese

4 thin slices smoked salmon, about 4 oz.

2 inch piece cucumber, sliced

2 tablespoons Coleslaw (page 59), optional

serves 4

Spread all the bagel halves with the cream cheese. Put a slice of smoked salmon and some cucumber slices on four of the bagel halves. Divide the coleslaw, if using, between them, then top with the bagel lids.

Cut each bagel in half. Wrap in plastic wrap or foil and store in the refrigerator until ready to pack.

VARIATIONS

- Vegetable and Nut Pâté (page 52) with shredded lettuce.
- Cream cheese topped with halved grapes.
- Vegetable Burger (page 109) with a little Salsa (page 96) or sliced tomato.
- Thinly sliced organic ham with cream cheese and a spread of Walnut Pesto (page 86).

HUMMUS PITA POCKETS

PREPARATION TIME 15 minutes

4 whole-wheat pita breads

4 tablespoons Hummus (page 51)

½ romaine lettuce, roughly shredded

3-inch piece cucumber, thinly sliced

3–4 medium tomatoes, thinly sliced

1 carrot, grated

2 tablespoons grated Cheddar cheese

serves 4

Warm the pita breads in a toaster or under a hot broiler for 1 minute. Let cool slightly, then split them. Put 1 tablespoon hummus in each one. Half fill with lettuce, then add some cucumber and tomato slices and grated carrot. Add some cheese, then wrap in plastic wrap or foil and store in the refrigerator until ready to pack.

CHICKEN & AVOCADO ROLL

PREPARATION TIME 12–15 minutes

1 large avocado, peeled, pit removed, and flesh sliced

2 teaspoons freshly squeezed lemon juice

1 medium tomato, seeded and finely chopped

4 whole-wheat rolls, cut in half

2–3 tablespoons low-fat cream cheese

1 Boston lettuce, rinsed

4 oz. thinly sliced roast organic chicken

serves 4

Put the avocado slices and lemon juice in a small bowl and mash to a rough puree with a fork. Add the tomato and mix well.

Spread each half of the rolls with a little cream cheese. Put a couple of lettuce leaves and 1 to 2 slices of chicken on top of 4 of the halves. Top with a spoonful of the avocado mixture and put the bread lid on top. Press lightly together, then wrap in plastic wrap or foil and store in the refrigerator until ready to pack.

SALADS

These salads are delicious, packed with nutrients, and a great alternative to sandwiches. They also make excellent suppers. On those really busy days when you don't have time to think, why not make a large salad for supper and set some aside for lunch the next day?

TUNA PASTA SALAD

PREPARATION TIME
15–20 minutes
COOKING TIME
12–15 minutes

3½ oz. whole-wheat pasta, such as penne

1 red onion, thinly sliced

3 celery stalks, chopped

1 carrot, grated

¼ cup raisins

3 inch piece cucumber, chopped

¼ cup cooked corn kernels

14 oz. canned tuna in spring water, drained and flaked

6 tablespoons reduced-calorie mayonnaise

6 tablespoons thick plain yogurt

to serve

salad leaves

8 oz. small vine-ripened plum tomatoes, cut in half

serves 4–6

Cook the pasta in a large saucepan of boiling water for 12 to 15 minutes, or according to the instructions on the package, until "al dente" (cooked but with a slight bite to it). Drain, refresh under cold running water, and transfer to a large bowl.

Cut the onion slices in half to form half moons, then add to the bowl along with the celery, carrot, raisins, cucumber, corn, and drained tuna.

Mix the mayonnaise with the yogurt and add it to the salad. Stir gently until well coated. (You can make the recipe up to this point and store, covered, in the refrigerator for up to 2 days.)

To serve, line a lunch box or airtight container with the salad leaves, put a serving of the pasta salad on top, and scatter over a few halved tomatoes.

COUSCOUS SALAD

Every busy parent should keep a packet of couscous in the cupboard. It couldn't be quicker or easier to prepare, it can be eaten hot or cold in a number of different ways, and children really like its texture.

PREPARATION TIME 15–18 minutes

2 cups instant couscous

1 red bell pepper, seeded and chopped

1 yellow bell pepper, seeded and chopped

1 lb. vine-ripened tomatoes, finely chopped

3-inch piece cucumber, finely chopped

¼ cup raisins

⅓ cup pecans, toasted

¼ cup black olives, pitted and cut in half

2 tablespoons chopped fresh flat-leaf parsley

2 tablespoons chopped fresh mint leaves

3 tablespoons extra virgin olive oil

2 tablespoons freshly squeezed lemon juice

1 teaspoon honey, warmed

1 tablespoon balsamic vinegar

freshly ground black pepper

serves 4–6

Put the couscous in a large heatproof bowl and cover with 1 cup boiling water. Stir, cover, and let stand for 10 minutes.

Fluff up the couscous with a fork. Add the bell peppers, tomatoes, cucumber, raisins, pecans, olives, and herbs, and mix well. (You can make the recipe up to this point and store, covered, in the refrigerator for up to 2 days.)

Put the oil, lemon juice, honey, vinegar, and pepper in a screwtop jar and shake until well mixed. Pour it over the couscous and stir well. Transfer to a lunch box or airtight container.

SAFFRON FISH PILAF

This protein-packed salad uses basmati rice, which has the added advantage of releasing its sugars into the blood stream at a very slow rate throughout the afternoon.

PREPARATION TIME
15 minutes
COOKING TIME 45 minutes

2 teaspoons virgin olive oil

1 onion, chopped

2–3 garlic cloves, crushed (optional)

¾ cup brown basmati rice, rinsed

¼ teaspoon saffron powder

3–4 cups vegetable broth

12 oz. white fish, such as cod, skinned if necessary and cut into small pieces

3½ oz. undyed smoked haddock fillet, skinned and cut into small pieces (optional)

1 lb. tomatoes, chopped

⅓ cup frozen peas

⅓ cup frozen corn kernels

1 tablespoon chopped fresh cilantro

2 hard-cooked eggs (page 41), shelled and quartered

freshly ground black pepper

serves 4–6

Heat the oil in a large skillet, add the onion and garlic, if using, and sauté gently for 3 minutes. Add the rice and continue to sauté, stirring, for 2 minutes. Add the saffron powder and stir well. Add half the broth, bring to a boil, then reduce the heat and simmer gently for about 25 minutes, stirring occasionally, adding more broth as the broth is absorbed by the rice.

Add the fish, tomatoes, peas, and corn, stir well, and cook for 10 minutes. Add the cilantro and pepper, to taste, then cook for another 5 minutes until the rice is tender.

Top with the hard-cooked egg, then transfer to an airtight container or lunch box.

VARIATION

• Replace the fish with 10 oz. chopped ham and ½ cup chopped fresh pineapple.

COLESLAW

Storebought coleslaw tends to contain (among other things) the minimum amount of vegetables and lots of high fat, watered down mayonnaise. This homemade version is quite the opposite. It is so full of fruit and vegetables that it is almost an entrée in itself. The walnuts add extra protein and essential fatty acids.

PREPARATION TIME 20 minutes

2 red apples

¼ cup freshly squeezed orange or lemon juice

1 lb. white cabbage

1 onion, thinly sliced or grated

6 oz. carrots, grated

3 celery stalks, finely chopped

¼ cup raisins

¼ cup walnuts, chopped (optional)

6 tablespoons sour cream

freshly ground black pepper

serves 4–6

Cut the apples into quarters and core them. Grate them into a large bowl, add 2 tablespoons of the orange or lemon juice, and stir until well coated.

Cut the cabbage into wedges and discard the outer leaves and hard central core. Wash thoroughly, then shred finely. (Use the shredding attachment on a food processor to save time.) Add it to the apple along with the onion, carrots, celery, raisins, and walnuts, if using. Stir well.

In a separate bowl, mix the sour cream with the remaining orange or lemon juice and pepper, to taste. Add it to the vegetables and stir well. The coleslaw can be stored in an airtight container in the refrigerator for up to 2 days.

VARIATION

• Try adding corn kernels, shredded red and green bell peppers, and grated celeriac to the mixture.

OATY CHOCOLATE CRUNCHIES

There is nothing wrong with a little chocolate now and again, especially when it's high in iron-rich cocoa solids and melted over nutritious nuts, seeds, and oats.

PREPARATION TIME
10–12 minutes

3½ oz. semisweet chocolate (at least 70 percent cocoa solids)

1½ cups Granola (page 32)

12 paper cupcake liners

makes 12

Break the chocolate into small pieces and put them in a heatproof bowl. Place the bowl over a saucepan of gently simmering, not boiling, water. Make sure the bottom of the bowl doesn't touch the water. Melt the chocolate gently, stirring occasionally, until it is smooth. Remove the bowl from the pan.

Add the granola to the melted chocolate and mix thoroughly. Put about 1 tablespoon of the mixture into each cupcake liner. Leave for 1 hour until set before serving. Store in an airtight container for up to 1 week.

Did You Know?

Chocolate with a high cocoa solid content (at least 70 percent) contains immune-boosting antioxidants, as well as more iron and twice the magnesium levels of milk chocolate. It also triggers the release of serotonin and endorphin, which make us feel happier. But go easy, because despite its good points, chocolate is still high in fat.

APRICOT & WALNUT BARS

These cereal bars are much lower in fat than most commercial versions. The dried apricots and oats make them high in fiber and very filling. The walnuts add a lovely extra crunch, as well as protein and omega 3 fatty acids.

PREPARATION TIME 12 minutes
COOKING TIME 20–25 minutes

1 stick sunflower margarine

2 tablespoons light brown sugar

5 tablespoons golden syrup

1¼ cups old-fashioned rolled oats

⅓ cup dried apricots, chopped

⅓ cup walnuts, chopped

a baking pan, 8 inches square, lightly greased

serves 10

Put the margarine, sugar, and golden syrup in a large saucepan and heat gently, stirring occasionally, until the margarine has melted and the sugar has dissolved.

Remove the pan from the heat and add the oats, apricots, and walnuts. Stir well until thoroughly mixed, then press into the prepared baking pan with the back of a spoon.

Bake in a preheated oven at 350°F for 20 to 25 minutes until golden and firm to the touch. Remove from the oven and let cool before cutting into bars. Leave until completely cold, then remove them from the pan. Store in an airtight container for up to 5 days.

GINGERBREAD PEOPLE

Younger children will love to help you make these. They will be far lower in saturated fat, sugar, and additives than most cookies you are likely to buy at the supermarket. Ground ginger is rich in iron, as are the ground almonds, which are also high in calcium and magnesium (both needed for strong bone development) and zinc, which supports the immune system and builds resistance to disease.

PREPARATION TIME
20 minutes
COOKING TIME 10–12 minutes

1½ cups self-rising flour

½ teaspoon baking soda

1–2 teaspoons ground ginger

2 teaspoons light brown sugar

1 tablespoon ground almonds

4 tablespoons sunflower margarine

⅓ cup golden syrup

currants, for decorating

shaped cookie cutter

2–3 baking trays, lightly greased

makes 12

Sift the flour, baking soda, and ground ginger into a large bowl and stir in the sugar and ground almonds.

Melt the margarine and golden syrup in a heavy-based saucepan over gentle heat, stirring occasionally, until melted. Remove the pan from the heat and gradually add to the flour, mixing with a wooden spoon, to give a soft but not sticky dough. Knead gently just to bring the dough together.

Transfer the dough to a lightly floured counter and roll out to a thickness of ¼ inch. Using a shaped cookie cutter, cut out people shapes, then carefully lift them onto a baking tray using a spatula. Press in a few currants for buttons, then mark the mouth and eyes with a small sharp knife.

Bake in a preheated oven at 375°F for 10 to 12 minutes until golden brown. Let cool for 5 minutes on the baking trays, then transfer them carefully to a wire rack and let cool completely. Store in an airtight container for up to 1 week.

OATMEAL CHOCOLATE CHIP COOKIES

Oatmeal is high in a number of minerals including zinc, iron, calcium, and magnesium. It's also a good source of B vitamins, needed for everything from energy production to good brain function and the healthy development of nerve tissues. The combination of the oatmeal and the whole-wheat flour will ensure that the sugars from this snack are released into the blood stream at a slow, steady, and sustained pace.

PREPARATION TIME 12–15 minutes
COOKING TIME 12–15 minutes

1 cup whole-wheat flour

1 cup medium oatmeal

2 tablespoons light brown sugar

⅓ cup raisins

2 oz. semisweet chocolate (at least 70 percent cocoa solids), finely chopped

1 egg

2 tablespoons sunflower oil

2–3 tablespoons milk

2 baking trays, lightly greased

makes 12–14

Put the flour and oatmeal in a large bowl and stir in the sugar, raisins, and chocolate. Put the egg in a small bowl and beat in the oil and milk. Stir the egg mixture into the flour and mix to form a stiff dough.

Put small spoonfuls of the mixture on the baking trays, spacing them well apart. Flatten slightly with the prongs of a fork, then bake in a preheated oven at 350°F for 12 to 15 minutes until golden.

Let cool on the baking trays for 2 to 3 minutes, then transfer to a wire rack and let cool completely. The cookies can be stored in an airtight container for up to 5 days.

EASY CARROT CUPCAKES

These are a firm favorite with my children and they couldn't be easier to make. The nuts add an irresistible crunch to what is otherwise a really moist, soft cake.

PREPARATION TIME 15 minutes
COOKING TIME 15–25 minutes

2 eggs

½ cup sugar

1¼ cups grated carrot

⅓ cup freshly squeezed orange juice

2 teaspoons finely grated unwaxed orange zest

¾ cup pecans or walnuts, roughly chopped

½ teaspoon ground cinnamon

½ cup sunflower oil

2¼ cups self-rising flour, sifted

topping (optional)

6 oz. cream cheese

1 tablespoon finely grated unwaxed lemon zest

1½ cups confectioners' sugar

a 12-hole muffin pan, lined with 9 paper muffin liners

makes 9 cupcakes

Put the eggs, sugar, carrot, orange juice and zest, nuts, cinnamon, oil, and flour in a large bowl, and stir with a wooden spoon until well mixed.

Spoon the mixture into the paper liners, until three-quarters full. Bake in a preheated oven at 350°F for 40 minutes until cooked. Test by inserting a clean skewer into the center of a cake; it should come out clean. Remove from the oven and let cool.

To make the topping, if using, put the cream cheese and lemon zest in a bowl and beat with a wooden spoon until soft. Gradually beat in the confectioners' sugar to form a stiff icing. Spread on top of the cooled cakes. Store in an airtight container for up to 3 days.

DOUBLE CHOCOLATE & HAZELNUT BROWNIES

Everyone loves chocolate brownies. These use sunflower margarine instead of butter to lower the saturated fat content, cocoa powder and semisweet chocolate to boost the iron content, and chopped hazelnuts to increase the amount of essential fatty acids and minerals. Serve as a tea-time treat, in packed lunches, at parties, or as a dessert with fresh raspberries.

PREPARATION TIME
12–15 minutes
COOKING TIME 25 minutes

3½ oz. semisweet chocolate (at least 70 percent cocoa solids)

2 tablespoons milk

1 stick sunflower margarine

1 cup raw sugar

2 eggs, beaten

⅓ cup unsweetened cocoa powder

½ cup self-rising flour

⅓ cup chopped hazelnuts

a baking pan, 8 inches square, lightly greased and completely lined with nonstick parchment paper

makes 9 squares

Break the chocolate into small pieces and put them in a heavy-based saucepan. Add the milk and heat gently, stirring, until the chocolate is melted and smooth. Remove the pan from the heat and let cool slightly.

Put the margarine and sugar in a large bowl and beat with a hand-held electric beater or a wooden spoon until the mixture is light and fluffy. Beat in the eggs a little at a time, beating well after each addition, until blended. Sift the cocoa powder into the egg mixture and stir gently until mixed. Pour in the melted chocolate and stir well.

Gently stir in the flour and hazelnuts—do not beat or overmix or the brownies will be dry. Spoon the mixture into the prepared pan and smooth the top. Bake in a preheated oven at 325°F for about 25 minutes. To test if they are cooked, insert a skewer into the center; it should come out almost clean with a slightly sticky feel.

Remove from the oven and let cool before marking into squares. Store in an airtight container for up to 1 week, or wrap and freeze for up to 1 month.

APPLE TEA BREAD

This tea bread is so versatile. It is great eaten just as it is for picnics or car journeys, but it is also delicious served as a quick snack with some Cheddar cheese and halved grapes on top. Alternatively, serve it warm for dessert topped with a little sour cream.

PREPARATION TIME
15 minutes
COOKING TIME
45–50 minutes

1⅓ cups whole-wheat flour

½ cup light brown sugar

2 teaspoons baking powder, sifted

½ teaspoon baking soda

1 teaspoon ground cinnamon

½ teaspoon freshly grated nutmeg

1 large apple, cored and grated

⅓ cup raisins

⅓ cup walnuts, chopped

7 tablespoons unsalted butter, melted

1 egg, beaten

about ⅓ cup apple juice

a loaf pan, 9 x 3 inches, lightly greased and lined with nonstick parchment paper

makes 1 loaf

Put the flour, sugar, baking powder, baking soda, and spices in a large bowl and mix. Stir in the grated apple, raisins, and walnuts. Mix well.

Mix in the melted butter, then stir in the beaten egg and the apple juice to give a soft dropping consistency. Add a little more apple juice if the mixture is too stiff.

Spoon the mixture into the prepared pan and bake in a preheated oven at 350°F for 45 to 50 minutes until cooked. To check, insert a skewer into the center of the loaf; it should come out clean. Remove from the oven and let cool in the pan. Serve in slices. Store in an airtight container for up to 5 days, or wrap and freeze for up to 1 month.

VARIATION
- Replace the walnuts with slivered almonds and sprinkle some more over the top before baking. Use other dried fruit, such as chopped apricots, in place of the raisins.

DATE BARS

Dates are naturally sweet and yet they will release their sugars at a far slower, steadier pace into the blood stream than other more refined sugars.

PREPARATION TIME
12–15 minutes
COOKING TIME
25–30 minutes

12 oz. pitted dates

1¼ cups whole-wheat flour

1¼ cups old-fashioned rolled oats

12 tablespoons sunflower margarine

a baking pan, 8 inches square, lightly greased and lined with nonstick parchment paper

makes 9

Put the dates and 1 cup cold water in a heavy-based saucepan and bring to a boil. Reduce the heat and simmer gently for 5 to 8 minutes until the dates are very soft. Beat with a wooden spoon or transfer to a blender and process to form a puree. Let cool.

Sift the flour into a large bowl and stir in the oats. Add the sunflower margarine and rub it in with the tips of your fingers until the mixture resembles fine bread crumbs. Add 3 to 4 tablespoons cold water and mix with a round-bladed knife to form a soft dough.

Put half the dough in the prepared pan and press out to cover the base. Spread the date puree over the top. Put the remaining dough on top and press out carefully to cover the dates. Bake in a preheated oven at 375°F for 25 to 30 minutes until golden. Remove from the oven and let cool before marking into 9 squares. Once cold, cut out the squares and remove them from the pan. Store in an airtight container for up to 1 week.

FRESH FRUIT DRINKS

All too often storebought drinks and syrups are laden with sugar to give them taste, additives to give them shelf life, and colorings to give them "child appeal." These recipes use the natural sugars and colors of fresh fruit and vegetables instead, and they're packed with naturally occurring vitamins and minerals.

PEAR & GINGER JUICE

Pear is very gentle on the digestive system and ginger is an effective remedy against nausea and travel sickness, so this is a great drink to take on journeys or to give to your child after a stomach upset.

PREPARATION TIME 5 minutes

12 oz. ripe pears, peeled, cored, and chopped

1 large orange, broken into segments

1-inch piece ginger, chopped

2 tablespoons crushed ice, to serve (optional)

serves 2

Push the pears, orange, and ginger through a juicer. Put 1 tablespoon crushed ice, if using, in each of 2 tall glasses, pour the juice over the top, and serve.

APPLE & CARROT JUICE

This is high in soluble fiber, which is necessary for a healthy digestive system, and full of immune-boosting antioxidants.

PREPARATION TIME
8 minutes

3 carrots, chopped

2 eating apples, peeled, cored, and chopped

2 tablespoons crushed ice, to serve (optional)

serves 2

Push the carrot and apple pieces through a juicer. Put 1 tablespoon crushed ice, if using, in each of 2 tall glasses, pour the juice over the top, and serve.

LEMON CORDIAL

Packed with vitamin C, this is a great immune-boosting drink.

PREPARATION TIME
15 minutes

freshly squeezed juice and zest of 6 unwaxed lemons

2 cups unrefined granulated sugar

to serve

lemon slices

ice cubes (optional)

makes 2 quarts

Put the lemon juice in a large bowl, add the sugar, and stir well.

Put the lemon zest and 5 cups cold water in a saucepan and bring to a boil. Reduce the heat and simmer for 3 minutes. Strain through a fine mesh strainer onto the lemon juice and sugar mixture and stir until the sugar has dissolved. Discard the zest.

Cover loosely and let cool completely. Pour the cordial into 2 sterilized screwtop bottles (page 4) and close securely.

To serve, pour a small amount of cordial into a tall glass and dilute to taste with cold water. Add slices of lemon and ice cubes, if liked.

Store in the refrigerator for up to 2 weeks.

MILK SHAKES

Milk shakes are almost an entire meal in themselves and provide the perfect opportunity to increase your child's fruit intake. Here are a few delicious ideas that can be whizzed up in minutes. Don't be afraid to experiment by adding any type of soft fruit that you know your child likes.

CHOCOLATE MONKEY MILK SHAKE

Bananas are the perfect fast food. They are satisfyingly filling, release their sugars slowly into the blood stream, and are high in potassium and vitamin B6.

PREPARATION TIME 5 minutes

1¼ cups low-fat milk (use whole milk for children under 5)

¾ cup plain yogurt

2 ripe bananas, sliced

2 tablespoons crushed ice (optional)

2 teaspoons finely grated semisweet chocolate (at least 70 percent cocoa solids)

serves 2

Put the milk, yogurt, and bananas in a blender and process until smooth. Put 1 tablespoon crushed ice, if using, in each of 2 tall glasses and pour the milk shake over the top. Sprinkle with the grated chocolate and serve immediately.

HONEY, APPLE, & BANANA SHAKE

PREPARATION TIME 5 minutes

2 ripe bananas, sliced

1 cup plain yogurt

2 teaspoons honey

¼ cup apple juice

ice cubes, to serve (optional)

serves 2

Put the bananas, yogurt, honey, and apple juice in a blender and process until smooth. Pour into 2 tall glasses, add ice cubes, if using, and serve immediately.

RASPBERRY MILK SHAKE

PREPARATION TIME 5 minutes

⅔ cup low-fat milk (use whole milk for children under 5)

½ cup plain yogurt

½ cup raspberries

2 teaspoons high fruit content raspberry jam (optional)

2 tablespoons crushed ice, to serve

serves 2

Put the milk, yogurt, raspberries, and jam, if using, in a blender and process for 1 minute. Put 1 tablespoon crushed ice in each of 2 tall glasses and pour in the milk shake. Serve immediately.

VARIATION
- Use pitted, canned black cherries or fresh blackberries or strawberries in place of the raspberries.

Did You Know?

Raspberries contain ellagic acid, which is known to help protect against cancer. They are also packed with vitamin C.

LUNCHES & SUPPERS

The food industry spends millions of dollars each year convincing both us and our children that the foods they produce are nutritious and desirable. Consequently, fish sticks, burgers, baked beans, chicken nuggets, pizza, and fries have become the staple foods on offer to our children, whether it's at home, in restaurants, daycares, or schools. The high fat, salt, and sugar content of these foods makes them a delight to a child's taste buds and they are therefore readily accepted. This only serves to confirm the belief that kids need to eat these foods. However, a closer look at the content and nutritional value of these products shows that nothing could be further from the truth.

BURGERS AND SAUSAGES A recent report by The Food Commission in the U.K. found that most frozen burgers are fatty, over-salted products pumped up with non-meat fillers, water, and flavorings. Some burgers contain 6 teaspoons of artery clogging saturated fat—even after being broiled. The survey also found many companies used cheap filling agents to pad out the meat, and chemicals to increase the amount of water in the product. The same is true of many sausages. Burgers and sausages, especially the cheaper varieties, are often made from the very last scraps of meat from a carcass that can legally be used.

FISH STICKS Fresh fish coated in bread crumbs or a little batter sounds a healthy choice. However, many versions contain unrecognizable fish pulp made from fish scraps, which is blended with salt and other additives, then reformed into the shape of a fish stick.

These are then coated in bread crumbs or batter, which may also contain additives and only serves to increase the fat content.

CHICKEN NUGGETS The meat used in chicken nuggets is invariably low-grade mulch from intensively produced poultry, bound with chemical additives and cheap fillers. The coating retains the fat from the meat, even if it is broiled. Some varieties have been found to contain only one-third meat and two-thirds coating.

PIZZA Most commercially prepared pizzas consist of a base of highly refined dough topped with over-sweetened tomato paste, a handful of processed cheese, and the occasional slice of very salty, additive-packed processed meat. They are often devoid of vegetables and, although filling, offer very little nutritional value.

FRENCH FRIES Deep-fried French fries are very high in fat. Even oven fries can contain up to 40 percent fat. Also, fast-food fries are usually loaded with unhealthful trans fat.

BAKED BEANS The beans themselves contain fiber, protein, and other valuable vitamins. However, most commercially prepared baked beans are coated in a sauce that is excessively high in both sugar and salt.

READY MEALS Although very convenient to buy, the nutritional content of ready meals is often very low. Much of the food's natural flavor is lost during processing, so extra fat, salt, and sugar are added to compensate. The shelf life is prolonged with preservatives and the appearance enhanced by adding colorings.

REAL ALTERNATIVES
whole-wheat spaghetti mixed with peas and corn, a chopped fresh tomato, a little olive oil, and some grated Cheddar cheese sprinkled over • Dippy Eggs (page 41) with whole-wheat toast • Homemade Baked Beans (page 76) mixed with canned tuna or salmon, served on whole-wheat toast • blend a can of chopped tomatoes with a can of tuna and a can of butter beans, heat, and serve with crusty whole-wheat bread • hard-cooked egg, bacon, and tomato on toast • add some frozen mixed vegetables to a saucepan of boiling pasta a couple of minutes before the pasta is cooked, drain, and mix with some pesto and sour cream • toast a whole-wheat pita bread and fill with sliced avocado and tomato and organic sliced ham • heat a flour tortilla and fill with mashed avocado, cold shredded chicken, some sour cream, and chopped tomato

CREAMY POTATO & BROCCOLI SOUP

Broccoli is one of the best cancer-fighting vegetables you can eat. It is also packed with immune-boosting phytochemicals and is an excellent source of vitamin C and beta-carotene.

PREPARATION TIME 12–15 minutes
COOKING TIME about 30 minutes

1 tablespoon olive oil

1 large onion, chopped

2 garlic cloves, crushed

2 lb. potatoes, cut into 1-inch cubes

3 cups organic vegetable broth

1¼ lb. broccoli, divided into florets and chopped

½–⅔ cup milk

freshly ground black pepper

serves 4

Heat the olive oil in a large, heavy-based saucepan. Add the onion and garlic, and sauté gently for 5 to 8 minutes until soft but not browned. Add the cubed potatoes and cook for a further 3 minutes.

Pour in the broth, bring to a boil, cover, and simmer for 15 minutes. Add the broccoli and cook for another 5 to 8 minutes until the vegetables are soft. Remove from the heat and let cool slightly.

Transfer the contents of the pan to a blender or food processor and blend, in batches if necessary, to form a smooth puree. Return the puree to the rinsed pan and stir in enough milk to give a slightly thick soup. Add pepper to taste, and reheat gently, stirring occasionally, until hot. Ladle into warm soup bowls to serve.

PUMPKIN SOUP

This is a really filling, warming soup that is perfect for chilly autumn days. It is packed full of beta-carotene, a powerful antioxidant that will boost the immune system and lower the risk of many cancers. Pumpkin is also easy to digest, so it's great for kids recovering from short bouts of illness.

PREPARATION TIME
15–18 minutes
COOKING TIME
about 30 minutes

1 pie pumpkin, about 2 lb.

1 tablespoon olive oil

1 potato, about 6 oz., diced

1 onion, chopped

1–2 garlic cloves, crushed

1 teaspoon ground cumin

4 cups organic vegetable or chicken broth

1 tablespoon chopped fresh sage leaves

⅔ cup sour cream

to serve, your choice of:

freshly grated nutmeg

finely grated Gruyère or Cheddar cheese

roasted pumpkin seeds (see cook's tips)

croutons (see cook's tips)

serves 6

Using a large sharp knife, cut the pumpkin into small wedges, then scoop out the seeds (see cook's tips). Using a small sharp vegetable knife, peel and discard the skin, then cut the flesh into small pieces.

Heat the oil in a heavy-based saucepan, add the potato, onion, and garlic, and cook gently, stirring occasionally, for 5 to 8 minutes until the vegetables are softened but not browned. Sprinkle in the ground cumin and cook for 1 minute more.

Add the broth, chopped pumpkin, and sage to the pan. Bring to a boil, reduce the heat, cover, and simmer gently for 20 to 25 minutes until the pumpkin is soft.

Remove the pan from the heat and let cool slightly. Transfer the mixture to a blender or food processor and blend, in batches if necessary, to form a smooth puree.

Return the puree to the rinsed pan and heat gently. Stir in the sour cream, then ladle into warm soup bowls. Serve sprinkled with a little freshly grated nutmeg, some grated cheese, roasted pumpkin seeds, or croutons.

COOK'S TIPS

- To roast the pumpkin seeds, first rinse them, discarding any pith around them. Spread them out in an even layer on a baking tray and let dry. Roast in a preheated oven at 375°F for 10 to 15 minutes, stirring occasionally, until golden.
- To make croutons, chop 2 slices of whole-wheat bread into small cubes. Heat 2 tablespoons olive oil in a heavy-based skillet, add the bread cubes, and cook over moderate heat, stirring frequently, for 5 to 8 minutes until golden and crisp. Drain on paper towels.

SARDINE BRUSCHETTA

These Italian-inspired toasted sandwiches are extremely versatile and make a delicious and quick lunch or supper dish.

PREPARATION TIME 5 minutes
COOKING TIME 2–3 minutes

4 oz. canned sardines

1 teaspoon balsamic vinegar

1 slice of whole-wheat bread, lightly toasted

1 tablespoon finely grated Cheddar cheese (optional)

3–4 cherry tomatoes, cut in half

serves 1

Put the sardines and balsamic vinegar in a bowl and mash with a fork. Pile the sardines on top of the toasted bread and sprinkle with the grated cheese, if using.

Transfer to a broiler pan along with the tomatoes and cook under a preheated broiler for 2 to 3 minutes until the cheese is golden brown and the tomatoes are hot.

Put the tomatoes on top of the toast, cut it into fingers, and serve immediately.

HOMEMADE BAKED BEANS

Ready prepared baked beans are so cheap to buy that it may seem like madness to make your own. Until you inspect the label, that is. Most commercially prepared versions are extremely high in salt and sugar. Some cans contain as many as 4 teaspoons of sugar, and almost twice as much salt as a young child should eat in a whole day.

PREPARATION TIME 10 minutes
COOKING TIME 1–1¼ hours

four 15-oz. cans white beans, such as navy, cannellini, or borlotti, rinsed and drained

3 medium onions, finely chopped

4 garlic cloves, crushed

2 tablespoons olive oil

1–1½ teaspoons paprika

1½–2 tablespoons molasses

3 tablespoons tomato paste

4 teaspoons Worcestershire sauce (optional)

sea salt and freshly ground black pepper

toasted whole-wheat bread, to serve

a large bean pot or Dutch oven

serves 15–20

Put the beans in a large pot or Dutch oven, add all the remaining ingredients (except the toast), season lightly with salt and pepper, and cover with 2 cups boiling water. Mix well.

Cover and cook in a preheated oven at 350°F for 1 to 1¼ hours, stirring occasionally, until the sauce is thick and rich in taste and texture. Check the seasoning and add extra Worcestershire sauce, if necessary, and extra molasses if slightly bitter.

Serve immediately with freshly toasted whole-wheat bread.

COOK'S TIPS
- This may seem like a large quantity to make, but the beans freeze well. To freeze, let cool, then transfer to freezerproof containers. Freeze for up to 1 month.
- These beans would be an ideal accompaniment for broiled fish, chicken, or burgers (pages 106–109), or serve them on top of a baked sweet potato.

VARIATIONS
- Add some chopped fresh parsley or cilantro at the end of cooking.
- Add ½ teaspoon chile powder with the rest of the ingredients.
- Add some chopped broiled bacon, ham, or sliced premium-quality sausage at the end of cooking, and ensure that the meat or sausage is thoroughly cooked and piping hot before serving.

FRITTATA

PREPARATION TIME 5–8 minutes
COOKING TIME 15 minutes

2 oz. baby spinach leaves, about 2 handfuls

½ cup frozen peas

½ cup frozen corn

6 eggs

1 tablespoon olive oil

1 medium onion, thinly sliced

3 ripe tomatoes, finely chopped

1 tablespoon chopped fresh flat-leaf parsley,
cilantro, or basil leaves

sea salt and freshly ground black pepper

to serve

salad greens

whole-wheat bread

a nonstick skillet, 10 inches diameter

serves 4

Rinse the spinach, drain well, then put it in a saucepan with only the water clinging to the leaves. Cook over medium heat for 2 to 3 minutes until just wilted. Drain well, squeezing out any excess water, then chop it finely.

Put the frozen peas and corn in a saucepan of simmering water and cook for 3 minutes. Drain.

Put the eggs and 3 tablespoons cold water in a bowl and beat well. Add salt and pepper, to taste, then stir in the drained spinach.

Heat the oil in the skillet, add the onion, and sauté gently for about 5 minutes, stirring frequently, until it is softened but not browned. Pour the egg mixture into the pan and cook over medium heat for 3 minutes, drawing the egg mixture from the sides of the pan into the center using a fork. Add the peas, corn, and chopped tomatoes and continue cooking for 3 to 4 minutes until the eggs are set on the bottom. Put the pan under a preheated broiler and cook for 2 minutes until the top of the frittata is lightly browned.

Sprinkle with the chopped herbs and cut into wedges. Serve with salad greens and whole-wheat bread.

CHEESE & SPINACH SOUFFLÉS

PREPARATION TIME 12–15 minutes
COOKING TIME 25–30 minutes

8 oz. baby spinach leaves

2 tablespoons sunflower margarine

2 tablespoons whole-wheat flour

½ teaspoon powdered mustard

⅔ cup milk

½ teaspoon freshly grated nutmeg

3 eggs, separated

¼ cup grated sharp Cheddar cheese,
plus 2 teaspoons extra for sprinkling

freshly ground black pepper

a baking tray

6 ramekins, ⅔ cup each, lightly greased

serves 6

Preheat the oven to 350°F and put a baking tray in to heat up 5 minutes before cooking.

Rinse the spinach, drain well, then put it in a saucepan with only the water clinging to the leaves. Cook over medium heat for 2 to 3 minutes until just wilted. Drain well, squeezing out any excess water, then chop it finely.

Put the margarine in a heavy-based saucepan and melt over low heat. Using a wooden spoon, stir in the flour and powdered mustard and cook, stirring constantly, for 2 minutes. Remove the pan from the heat and gradually stir in the milk. Return the pan to the heat and cook, stirring, until the sauce is thick and smooth. Remove the pan from the heat and let cool slightly before adding the nutmeg and black pepper, to taste.

Add the egg yolks to the sauce one at a time, beating after each addition. Add the spinach, then stir in the cheese until melted.

Put the egg whites in a clean, grease-free bowl and beat until stiff peaks form. Gradually stir them into the sauce, but don't overmix. Put the prepared ramekins on the preheated baking tray and spoon the mixture into them, filling them about three-quarters full. Sprinkle the tops with the extra cheese and bake in the preheated oven for 20 to 25 minutes until well risen and golden brown. Serve immediately.

SIMPLE VEGETABLE QUICHE

Kids love quiche and this meat-free version is a great way to increase your child's vegetable intake. Almost any vegetables can be used, so be creative. The eggs provide an excellent source of protein, zinc, omega 3 fatty acids, and vitamins A, D, E, and B12.

PREPARATION TIME 15 minutes
COOKING TIME 1 hour

1 storebought whole-wheat pie crust

filling

3½ oz. broccoli, divided into small florets

1 tablespoon olive oil

1 onion, finely chopped

1 small red bell pepper, sliced into rings and seeded

1 medium carrot, grated

3 eggs

⅔ cup milk

¼ teaspoon freshly grated nutmeg

freshly ground black pepper

to serve (optional)

salad greens

boiled new potatoes

a baking tray

serves 6–8

Unwrap the pie crust and put it on a baking tray.

Steam the broccoli florets over a saucepan of gently simmering water for 3 minutes. Plunge them into cold water and drain well.

Heat the oil in a nonstick skillet, add the onion and fry gently for 5 minutes, stirring frequently. Transfer the onion to the pie crust, spreading it evenly over the base. Arrange the broccoli, bell pepper, and carrot on top of the onion. Put the eggs, milk, nutmeg, and black pepper in a bowl and beat well. Pour the mixture over the vegetables in the pie crust.

Bake in a preheated oven at 400°F for 15 minutes. Reduce the temperature to 350°F and continue to bake for about 20 minutes until the filling is set. Serve with salad and new potatoes, if liked.

COOK'S TIPS

* Ready-made whole-wheat pie crusts are available from health food stores.
* The cooked quiches can be frozen for up to 1 month.
* If you have the time to make the pastry shell yourself, make the pastry as directed on page 129, but omit the orange zest. Line a 10-inch diameter, loose-based tart pan with the rolled pastry. Put some crumpled foil in the pastry and bake in a preheated oven at 400°F for 15 minutes. Remove the foil and return the pastry shell to the oven for 5 minutes until set and lightly golden. Remove from the oven and let cool slightly. Continue as for the main recipe, above.

VARIATIONS

* Sprinkle the quiche with a little grated cheese just before baking.
* Add 1 tablespoon canned cannellini beans to the filling.
* Replace the broccoli and carrot with about 6 oz. finely chopped, well drained, blanched spinach and 2½ oz. crumbled goat cheese.

Did You Know?

According to recent government figures, the average British child eats fewer than half of the recommended five portions of fruit and vegetables a day, while almost 15 percent of children between the ages of five and 15 eat none.

PIZZA

There are so many reasons to make this, I don't know where to begin. Unlike most shop-bought pizzas, which consist of cardboard-like bases made from highly refined white flour and toppings of the smallest amount of tomato paste and a scattering of ready grated processed cheese, your homemade version will be both healthy and delicious.

PREPARATION TIME 15–20 minutes, plus 1 hour rising time
COOKING TIME 12–15 minutes

4 cups whole-wheat bread flour

1½ cups strong white bread flour, plus extra for sprinkling and dusting

1 sachet (3 teaspoons) quick-acting yeast

1½ teaspoons salt

1 tablespoon light brown sugar

3 tablespoons olive oil

about 2 cups tepid water

1 quantity Tomato Sauce (page 86)

fresh herbs, such as basil or oregano, to serve

toppings, your choice of:

Vegetables: baby asparagus spears, sliced tomatoes, thinly sliced zucchini, sliced bell peppers, corn kernels, peas, lightly steamed sugarsnap peas or snow peas, onion rings fried in a little olive oil until softened, lightly steamed broccoli florets, blanched spinach, sliced mushrooms, pitted olives

Meat: strips of ham,; broiled bacon, chopped; strips of prosciutto; shredded cooked chicken breast; slices of premium quality sausage

Fish: flaked canned tuna, smoked mackerel, flaked smoked salmon

Cheese: mozzarella, Cheddar, Gouda, Gruyère, goat cheese

2 baking trays, lightly greased

makes 8

Sift the flours into a large mixing bowl, adding the bran left in the sifter, and stir in the yeast, salt, and sugar. Make a well in the center, then pour in the olive oil and gradually add the tepid water, mixing the flour into the liquid. Add enough water to form a smooth and pliable dough.

Turn the dough out on to a lightly floured counter and knead for 10 minutes or until smooth and elastic. Put the dough in a clean, oiled bowl (or in an oiled plastic bag), cover, and let rise until doubled in size (about 1 hour).

Divide the dough into 8 equal balls and knead each one into a round. Roll each round on a lightly floured counter to a circle about 6 inches in diameter. Transfer the pizza bases to the baking trays.

Spread each base with 2 tablespoons of the tomato sauce, then add your choice of topping. Kids love to help put these together.

Bake in a preheated oven at 450°F for 12 to 15 minutes or until the bases are golden and the tops are bubbling. Sprinkle with fresh herbs, if using, and serve immediately.

COOK'S TIPS

- Any leftover dough can be wrapped and frozen for up to 1 month. Let the dough thaw thoroughly before shaping and using.
- Children love to "build" their own pizzas, so why not put bowls of different ingredients on the kitchen table and let them help themselves? This can work really well on special occasions such as parties or weekend suppers. When arranging the ingredients on the pizza base, start with the larger ingredients, such as strips of bell pepper, asparagus, or sliced tomato, and finish with the smaller ingredients, such as sliced mushrooms, and finally sprinkle with grated cheese.

VARIATION

- To make 8 to 10 mini party pizzas, use half the amount of dough given above (freeze the rest). Divide the dough into balls about the size of an egg. Roll them out on a lightly floured counter to form a circle about 3 inches diameter and ½ inch thick. Spread them with a little of the prepared tomato sauce, then let the children build up their own pizzas from the prepared toppings. Bake as in the main recipe for 8 to 10 minutes.

BAKED SWEET POTATOES WITH CHEESY LENTIL HASH & CRISPY BACON

Sweet potatoes and lentils are low-glycemic index foods, which means they release their sugars into the blood stream at a slow and steady rate, helping to keep children's energy levels constant. Lentils are also an excellent source of protein, iron, selenium, and potassium—a mineral which helps to counteract the effects of too much salt in the diet.

PREPARATION TIME
12 minutes
COOKING TIME 45–50 minutes

4 medium sweet potatoes

1 cup red split lentils

2–2½ cups organic vegetable broth

1–2 garlic cloves, crushed

1 onion, very finely chopped

2 celery stalks, very thinly sliced

1 tablespoon soy sauce

2 tablespoons tomato paste

6 slices lean bacon, broiled and chopped

¾ cup grated extra-sharp Cheddar cheese

an ovenproof dish

serves 4

Lightly prick the sweet potatoes with a fork and bake directly on the shelves of a preheated oven at 400°F for 35 to 40 minutes until soft when gently squeezed. Remove and leave until cool enough to handle.

Meanwhile, put the lentils in a saucepan, add the broth, and bring to a boil. Cover, reduce the heat, and simmer for about 20 minutes until soft. Add more broth or water if the lentils start to dry out.

Meanwhile, put the garlic, onion, celery, soy sauce, and 3 to 4 tablespoons water in a nonstick skillet and heat gently for about 10 minutes or until the vegetables are soft. Add them to the saucepan of cooked lentils along with the tomato paste, chopped bacon, and half the grated cheese. Mix well, then reheat gently, stirring occasionally, until hot.

Cut the cooked sweet potatoes in half. Put them in an ovenproof dish and top with the lentil mixture. Sprinkle with the remaining cheese and cook under a preheated hot broiler for 10 minutes or until the cheese is golden and bubbling. Serve hot.

COOK'S TIP

• To cook the sweet potatoes in a microwave, wrap them in paper towels and cook each one on HIGH for 4 to 4½ minutes. Let stand for 1 minute before topping with the lentils and broiling as in the main recipe. If you cook more than 1 potato at a time, increase the cooking time accordingly.

VARIATION

• Top the sweet potatoes with Homemade Baked Beans (page 76) instead of the lentils.

WARM POTATO SALAD

This versatile salad can be eaten hot or cold, as a meal in itself or as an accompaniment to burgers or broiled chicken.

PREPARATION TIME
15 minutes
COOKING TIME 15–20 minutes

1 lb. boiling potatoes, unpeeled

1 tablespoon plain yogurt

1 tablespoon sour cream

1 garlic clove, crushed

½ cucumber, finely chopped

1 small red bell pepper, seeded and finely chopped

2 hard-cooked eggs, chopped (page 41)

serves 4

Boil the potatoes in a large saucepan of simmering water for 15 to 20 minutes until the potatoes are tender when pierced with a fork. Drain and let cool slightly. When cool enough to handle, cut them into 1-inch cubes and put them in a serving bowl.

Put the yogurt, sour cream, and garlic in a separate bowl and mix. Spoon the mixture over the potatoes, add the cucumber, pepper, and eggs and stir carefully. Serve hot or cold.

WALNUT PESTO

Walnuts are an excellent source of omega 3 fatty acids, which are important for healthy brain development and can help reduce the risk of heart disease.

PREPARATION TIME
8–10 minutes

¼ cup walnut halves

½ cup grated Parmesan cheese

1 cup fresh basil leaves

3 garlic cloves, crushed

⅓–½ cup extra virgin olive oil

16 oz. freshly cooked pasta, to serve

serves 4

Put the walnuts in a food processor and grind to a fine meal. Add the cheese, basil, and garlic, and blend for 2 minutes. With the machine running, gradually add the oil through the feed tube and blend to a smooth, slightly grainy paste. Add more oil, if necessary. Spoon the pesto into a sterilized jar (page 4) and store, covered, in the refrigerator for up to 5 days.

To serve, stir into freshly cooked, hot pasta.

TOMATO SAUCE FOR PASTA

This sauce is so versatile that I suggest making four times the quantity here and freezing what you don't intend to use immediately. It can also be used on Pizza (page 82) or poured over broiled chicken or fish.

PREPARATION TIME 5–8 minutes
COOKING TIME 22 minutes

1 tablespoon olive oil

1 small onion, finely chopped

2 garlic cloves, crushed

1 red bell pepper, seeded and finely chopped

14 oz. canned chopped tomatoes

1–2 tablespoons tomato paste

1 teaspoon sugar

Worcestershire sauce, to taste (optional)

2 tablespoons chopped fresh basil leaves

sea salt and freshly ground black pepper

to serve

16 oz. freshly cooked pasta

freshly grated Parmesan cheese

serves 4

Heat the oil in a large, heavy-based saucepan, add the onion, garlic, and pepper, and sauté gently, stirring occasionally, for 8 to 10 minutes until softened but not browned. Add the tomatoes, tomato paste, sugar, and ¾ cup water. Bring to a boil, then reduce the heat and simmer gently for 10 to 12 minutes until reduced and thickened. Stir in the Worcestershire sauce, if using, basil, and salt and pepper, to taste.

Spoon the sauce over freshly cooked, hot pasta and serve immediately, sprinkled with some freshly grated Parmesan cheese.

COOK'S TIPS
• If your children prefer a smoother sauce, transfer the sauce to a food processor or blender and process briefly until smooth.
• Any leftover sauce can be poured into sterilized jars (page 4) and stored in the refrigerator for up to 1 week. Alternatively, pour the sauce into small, freezerproof containers and freeze for up to 2 months.

VARIATION
• To make a super-speedy ragù, you will need about 10 oz. lean ground beef (use soy meat for vegetarians). Gently heat 1 tablespoon olive oil in a nonstick saucepan, add the beef, and sauté gently for 5 minutes until sealed, then cook for a further 15 minutes, stirring frequently to break up any lumps. Add 2¼ cups of the prepared tomato sauce and heat through for about 5 minutes until piping hot. Serve with freshly cooked pasta, such as spaghetti.

TUSCAN TUNA & BEAN SAUCE

This is the fastest, easiest pasta sauce you can make, and it's so filling it can almost be served as a meal in itself with some crusty brown bread.

PREPARATION TIME 3–5 minutes
COOKING TIME 5 minutes

14 oz. canned chopped tomatoes

6½ oz. canned tuna in spring water, drained

10 oz. canned beans, such as red kidney, butter bean, or navy, drained and rinsed

⅓ cup organic vegetable broth

1 tablespoon chopped fresh cilantro

sea salt and freshly ground black pepper

1 lb. freshly cooked pasta, to serve

serves 6

Put the tomatoes, tuna, beans, broth, cilantro, and salt and pepper in a food processor and blend until smooth. Pour the mixture into a saucepan and heat, stirring occasionally, for about 5 minutes until piping hot. Alternatively, pour the mixture into a microwaveable bowl, cover with microwaveable wrap, pierce it, and heat on HIGH for 2 minutes. Stir and heat on HIGH for 1 minute more. Remove and let stand for 1 minute.

Spoon the sauce over freshly cooked, hot pasta, to serve.

COOK'S TIP

- For a chunkier sauce, simply put all the ingredients in a saucepan—there's no need to blend them. Stir well and heat gently until piping hot. Spoon over hot pasta, to serve.

ROASTED VEGETABLE SAUCE

I love this recipe because although there is a bit of work involved in chopping the vegetables, once they are prepared you simply pop them in the oven and forget about them for 40 minutes. You can serve the vegetables straight out of the oven, sprinkled with a little chopped ham and grated cheese.

PREPARATION TIME
12–15 minutes
COOKING TIME 35–45 minutes

1 sweet potato, cut into cubes

1 large carrot, sliced

1 onion, thickly sliced

2 zucchini, thickly sliced

1 red bell pepper, seeded and chopped

1 yellow bell pepper, seeded and chopped

2 celery stalks, sliced

12 cherry tomatoes, cut in half

4 garlic cloves, finely chopped

2 tablespoons olive oil

4 sprigs of fresh rosemary

14 oz. canned chopped tomatoes

sea salt and freshly ground black pepper

14 oz. freshly cooked pasta, to serve

serves 8

Put all the fresh vegetables and the garlic in a roasting pan and pour over the olive oil. Toss well to coat, then top with the rosemary sprigs. Roast in a preheated oven at 400°F for 30 to 40 minutes, stirring occasionally, until the vegetables are soft.

Remove from the oven and discard the rosemary. Let cool slightly, then stir in the canned tomatoes. Transfer the vegetables to a food processor and blend, in batches if necessary, until smooth. Add a little water if the sauce is too thick.

Transfer to a saucepan, season to taste with salt and pepper, then reheat gently for about 5 minutes until hot.

Spoon the sauce over freshly cooked, hot pasta, to serve.

COOK'S TIP

- When cold, spoon the sauce into small freezerproof containers. Label them and freeze for up to 2 months. Stir well when reheating.

VARIATION

- The sauce can also be served on top of broiled meat, burgers (pages 106–109), or baked potatoes.

FISH STICKS WITH SWEET POTATO FRIES & PEA PUREE

Here is a really healthy alternative to the all-time favorite, fish sticks, French fries, and peas. The fish sticks are made from 100 percent fresh fish coated in whole-wheat bread crumbs. The fries are replaced with vitamin- and fiber-packed sweet potatoes that are lightly baked in sunflower oil instead of being deep fried, while the homemade tomato ketchup adds a healthy dose of disease-fighting vitamins without all that unnecessary sugar.

PREPARATION TIME 15 minutes, plus 30 minutes chilling time
COOKING TIME 25 minutes

4 fillets of white fish, such as cod, haddock, or halibut, about 4 oz. each, skinned

2–3 tablespoons whole-wheat flour

1 egg, beaten

1½ cups fresh whole-wheat bread crumbs, made from at least 2-day-old bread

Real Tomato Ketchup (page 105), to serve

sweet potato fries

4 sweet potatoes, cut into wedges

2 tablespoons sunflower oil

pea puree

4 cups frozen peas

1 tablespoon sour cream

a baking tray, lightly greased

serves 4–6

Remove any fine bones from the fish and cut each fillet into 5 strips. Take 3 shallow dishes, put the flour in one, the beaten egg in another, and the bread crumbs in the third. First, coat a fish strip in the flour, then dip it into the egg, shaking off any excess, then coat it in bread crumbs. Transfer to a large plate. Repeat with the remaining fish strips until they are all coated. Lightly cover the coated fish with plastic wrap and chill in the refrigerator for at least 30 minutes.

To make the sweet potato fries, bring a large saucepan of water to a boil and add the wedges. Return the water to a boil and cook for 3 to 5 minutes until the sweet potatoes have softened. Drain well and transfer to a roasting pan. Pour over the oil and toss gently to coat. Cook on the top shelf of a preheated oven at 400°F for 15 minutes, turning the fries occasionally, until crisp and golden.

Meanwhile, put the fish sticks on the prepared baking tray and cook on the middle shelf of the preheated oven for about 10 minutes until golden.

To make the pea puree, put the peas in a microwaveable jug and add 2 tablespoons water. Microwave on HIGH for 6 minutes, then let stand for 1 minute. Add the sour cream and blend roughly with a hand-held blender. Alternatively, cook the peas in a saucepan of boiling water for 3 minutes. Drain well, transfer to a blender or food processor, add the sour cream, and blend to a puree.

Serve the fish sticks accompanied by the sweet potato fries and pea puree.

COOK'S TIP
- If you use fresh fish, you can freeze the coated sticks. Put them on a large, flat tray and open freeze until frozen. Pack them in a freezerproof container, label, date, and freeze for up to 1 month.

Did You Know?

Sweet potatoes contain vitamins A and C, they are a good source of fiber, which keeps the digestive tract healthy, and phytochemicals to protect against disease. They also release their sugars at a slower and steadier pace than regular potatoes, helping to keep energy levels constant and hunger pangs at bay.

FISH CAKES

Even children who turn up their noses at fish will usually eat fish cakes. These are packed with quality fish and are completely additive-free.

PREPARATION TIME 15 minutes, plus 30 minutes chilling time
COOKING TIME 25 minutes

14 oz. potatoes, cut into large chunks

1 lb. white fish fillet such as cod or haddock

1¼ cups milk

a handful of fresh flat-leaf parsley sprigs

1 bay leaf

1 tablespoon finely grated unwaxed lemon zest

2 tablespoons chopped fresh herbs, such as dill, parsley, or cilantro

2–3 tablespoons whole-wheat flour

2–3 tablespoons sunflower oil

sea salt and freshly ground black pepper

lemony green beans

5 oz. green beans

1 tablespoon freshly squeezed lemon juice

1 tablespoon extra virgin olive oil

makes 8 small fish cakes

Cook the potatoes in a large saucepan of boiling water for 15 minutes until tender. Drain and mash.

Meanwhile, rinse the fish and put it in a skillet with the milk, parsley sprigs, and bay leaf. Bring to a boil, then cover and simmer for 8 to 10 minutes until the fish is cooked and the flesh looks white. Remove the fish with a slotted spoon and transfer it to a large bowl. Let it cool slightly and when cool enough to handle, remove the skin and any bones and flake the flesh. Discard the cooking liquor.

Add the mashed potato, lemon zest, and chopped herbs to the fish. Season to taste with salt and pepper, then mix lightly. Using your hands, shape the mixture into 8 small fish cakes. Put the flour on a plate and dip the fish cakes in it, coating them evenly. Transfer the fish cakes to a plate, cover lightly with plastic wrap, and chill in the refrigerator for at least 30 minutes.

To make the lemony green beans, lightly steam the beans for about 5 minutes until cooked but still slightly crunchy. Drain well, transfer to a warmed serving bowl, and add the lemon juice, olive oil, and a sprinkling of salt. Toss well and cover to keep warm.

To cook the fish cakes, heat the sunflower oil in a skillet. Add the fish cakes and cook for 4 to 5 minutes on each side until golden brown, crisp, and piping hot. Serve immediately with the lemony green beans.

COOK'S TIPS
- Make double quantities of the fish cakes and freeze half of them after shaping. Ensure that you use fresh fish if freezing. Put them on a large, flat tray and open freeze until frozen, then pack in a freezerproof container, label, date, and freeze for up to 1 month.
- The fish cakes can be broiled or oven-baked instead of pan-fried. Brush lightly with a little oil, then cook under a preheated moderate broiler for 4 to 5 minutes on each side. Alternatively, put them on a baking tray, brush lightly with oil, and cook in a preheated oven at 375°F for 15 to 18 minutes until golden brown and piping hot.

VARIATIONS
- Replace the cod or haddock with salmon fillet.
- Add some chopped, cooked peeled shrimp, thawed if frozen.
- Serve the fish cakes with a little hot Roasted Vegetable Sauce (page 89) poured over the top.

FISH PIE

Protein, essential fatty acids, calcium, iron, fiber—you name it, this fish pie has got it. Every mouthful will help build fitter, stronger, healthier little bodies.

PREPARATION TIME 20 minutes
COOKING TIME 45–50 minutes

1 lb. potatoes, cut into large chunks

1 lb. cod or haddock fillet

1¾ cup milk

1 bay leaf

8 oz. canned tuna in spring water, drained

2 hard-cooked eggs, roughly chopped

6 oz. baby spinach leaves

1½ cups frozen peas

5 tablespoons sunflower oil

¼ cup flour

1 large leek, thinly sliced

½ cup grated Cheddar cheese (optional)

sea salt and freshly ground black pepper

honey-glazed carrots (optional)

about 14 oz. baby carrots

4 teaspoons honey

1 tablespoon unsalted butter

8 ramekins or small ovenproof dishes,
⅔ cup each, or 2 ovenproof dishes
2⅔ cups each

serves 8

Cook the potatoes in a large saucepan of boiling water for 15 minutes until tender. Drain and mash.

Rinse the cod or haddock and put it in a skillet. Add the milk and bay leaf and bring to a boil. Reduce the heat to a simmer and cook for 10 minutes. Remove the pan from the heat and strain off and reserve the cooking liquor. When the fish is cool enough to handle, remove the skin and any bones, then flake it. Flake the tuna into small pieces and add it to the cooked fish, along with the chopped eggs.

Meanwhile, put the spinach and peas in a steamer placed over gently simmering water and cook for 3 minutes. Squeeze out any excess water from the spinach and chop it. Stir the spinach and peas into the fish mixture, then divide it between the 8 ramekins.

Make the reserved cooking liquor up to 1⅔ cups, if necessary, with more milk or water. Heat ¼ cup oil in a small saucepan and stir in the flour. Cook over low heat, stirring, for 2 minutes. Remove the pan from the heat and gradually stir in the reserved cooking liquor. Return the pan to the heat and cook, stirring continuously, until the sauce thickens. Season to taste with salt and pepper, then pour the sauce over the fish in the ramekins.

Heat the remaining oil in a skillet. Add the sliced leek and cook for 5 minutes until softened. Divide the leeks between the ramekins, then top each one with the mashed potato. Sprinkle the tops with a little grated cheese, if using. Bake in a preheated oven at 375°F for 20 to 25 minutes until golden brown and bubbling.

Meanwhile, to make the honey-glazed carrots, if using, put the carrots in a steamer placed over gently simmering water and cook for 10 to 12 minutes until tender when pierced with a fork. Transfer the carrots to a warm serving bowl. Pour over the honey, add the butter, and stir until well coated.

Serve the fish pie immediately, accompanied by the warm carrots, if using.

COOK'S TIP

- To freeze the fish pies, assemble them, then let cool completely. Wrap well and freeze for up to 1 month. Remove the pies from the freezer the day before you want to cook them. Let them defrost thoroughly in the refrigerator, then pop them in the oven and cook as above.

CHICKEN & VEGETABLE FAJITAS

I don't know who loves this recipe the most in my family, the adults or the kids. It is full of fiber and foods that release their sugars at a steady pace into the blood stream—a great meal for ensuring your children's energy levels stay constant.

PREPARATION TIME 20 minutes
COOKING TIME 25 minutes

2 boneless, skinless chicken breasts, about 4 oz. each

1 tablespoon olive oil

1 yellow bell pepper, seeded and sliced

1 green bell pepper, seeded and sliced

14 oz. canned chopped tomatoes

1–2 garlic cloves, crushed

1 teaspoon mild chile powder (optional)

¼ teaspoon dried oregano

1 tablespoon tomato paste

14 oz. canned refried beans; or borlotti or pinto beans, rinsed, drained, and mashed

4 large wheat tortillas, 8 inches diameter

2–4 oz. extra-sharp Cheddar cheese

2 tablespoons sour cream

2 tablespoons chopped fresh cilantro

salsa

2 medium ripe, but still firm tomatoes, cut in half, seeded, and finely chopped

1 garlic clove, crushed

2 scallions, finely chopped (optional)

1–2 teaspoons freshly squeezed lemon juice

1 tablespoon chopped fresh cilantro

serves 4

To make the salsa, put the tomatoes, garlic, scallions, if using, lemon juice, and cilantro in a bowl. Stir well. Spoon into a small dish, cover, and set aside for 30 minutes for the flavors to develop. (If not using immediately, cover tightly and store in the refrigerator for up to 3 days. Stir before use.)

Rinse the chicken breasts and pat dry with paper towels. Heat a stovetop grill pan until smoking. Add the chicken to the pan and cook for 8 to 9 minutes on each side until thoroughly cooked. To check, pierce the thickest part with a skewer; the juices should run clear. If the juices run pink, continue to cook for a few minutes more. Remove the chicken from the pan and slice it thinly.

Heat the oil in a saucepan, add the peppers, and fry gently for 10 minutes until soft. Stir in the tomatoes, garlic, chile powder, if using, oregano, and tomato paste. Bring to a boil, reduce the heat, and simmer for about 10 minutes until the mixture has reduced slightly and thickened.

Put the beans in a small, heavy-based saucepan and heat gently, stirring frequently, until smooth and piping hot.

Wrap the tortillas in foil and heat in a preheated oven at 400°F for 6 to 7 minutes until soft and piping hot. Alternatively, heat in a microwave oven according to the directions on the package.

Spread each tortilla with a thick layer of mashed beans, 1 to 2 tablespoons of the tomato and pepper mixture, and one-quarter of the chicken slices. Sprinkle with grated cheese, salsa, sour cream, and cilantro. Roll up and serve immediately.

VARIATION
- For a vegetarian alternative, omit the chicken breast and add some sliced ripe avocado and cucumber.

Did You Know?
Tomatoes are an excellent source of lycopene, a powerful antioxidant that helps to protect against cancer and heart disease. The cooking process allows the body to absorb lycopene more easily, as does adding a little oil, so this recipe is perfect!

CHICKEN & PEA RISOTTO

Adults and children alike will love this protein-packed risotto. Skinless chicken contains very little fat and peas are a great source of immune-boosting vitamins A and C, as well as B vitamins—necessary for the development of a healthy nervous system and essential for growth—and folic acid.

PREPARATION TIME 10–12 minutes
COOKING TIME 30–35 minutes

3½–4 cups hot chicken broth

1 tablespoon sunflower oil

1 onion, finely chopped

2 garlic cloves, crushed

2 celery stalks, chopped

8 oz. boneless, skinless chicken breast, cut into bite-size cubes

1¼ cups risotto rice, such as arborio

1 small zucchini, grated

2 cups frozen peas

2 tablespoons sour cream

freshly ground black pepper

1 tablespoon chopped fresh flat-leaf parsley, to serve

serves 4–6

Put the broth in a saucepan and keep it at a gentle simmer.

Heat the oil in a large, heavy-based saucepan and add the onion, garlic, and celery. Cook gently for 5 minutes until softened and translucent but not browned. Add the chicken and cook for another 5 minutes, stirring frequently, until the chicken is sealed. Stir in the rice and cook for 1 to 2 minutes until the rice smells toasted and looks opaque.

Begin adding the broth, a large ladle at a time, stirring gently until each ladle has been absorbed by the rice. The rice should always be at a gentle simmer. Continue in this way for 10 minutes, then add the zucchini and peas to the pan. Continue adding broth as before until the rice is tender and creamy but the grains still firm, 5 to 10 minutes.

Taste and season with pepper, then stir in the sour cream. Cover and let rest for a few minutes. Serve sprinkled with chopped parsley.

VARIATION
• Use ham or smoked haddock fillet instead of the chicken.

Did You Know?
Frozen vegetables usually contain just as many vitamins and minerals as fresh ones. They are great for busy parents because they require no preparation and can be on the table in minutes.

READY, STEADY, GO STIR FRY

The key to a good stir fry is to make sure the vegetables retain some crunch (there's nothing kids hate more than soggy vegetables) and to cut the chicken into manageable strips.

PREPARATION TIME 15 minutes
COOKING TIME 12 minutes

2 garlic cloves, crushed

1 tablespoon sesame seeds

1–2 tablespoons soy sauce

2 teaspoons honey

2 boneless, skinless chicken breasts, about 4 oz. each

2 tablespoons peanut or sunflower oil

1 red bell pepper, seeded and thinly sliced

1 yellow bell pepper, seeded and thinly sliced

1 green bell pepper, seeded and thinly sliced

1 cup mini sweet corn (optional)

½ cup snow peas

8 oz. fine egg noodles

serves 4

Put the garlic, sesame seeds, soy sauce, honey, and 2 tablespoons water in a small bowl and mix well.

Cut the chicken into thin slices. Heat a wok until hot. Add the oil and heat until hot. Carefully add the chicken to the wok and stir fry for 3 minutes, stirring frequently, until the chicken is sealed. Add the peppers and fry for another 0 minutes, stirring frequently. Add the sweet corn and snow peas and fry for 2 minutes more.

Meanwhile, put the noodles in a saucepan of gently simmering water. Remove the pan from the heat and set aside for 3 minutes to let the noodles soften.

Add the soy sauce mixture to the wok, stir well, and cook for 2 to 3 minutes until the chicken is thoroughly cooked, but the vegetables still retain some bite.

Drain the noodles, divide them between 4 warmed bowls, top with the stir fry mixture, and serve immediately.

COOK'S TIPS
- It is important that the wok is preheated before adding the oil. This helps to prevent the chicken sticking to it and ensures that the chicken cooks quickly.
- Peanut or sunflower oil is better for stir frying than olive oil.

VARIATIONS
- Use strips of turkey or beef fillet instead of the chicken.
- Fish can also be used—try large peeled shrimp or strips of monkfish.
- Try other vegetables, such as asparagus, sugarsnap peas, sliced zucchini, sliced carrots, or broccoli florets.

Did You Know?

The color of a fruit or vegetable is often a good indication of its nutrient content. Green foods are often rich in the antioxidant vitamins A, C, and E. Red ones contain lycopene, a powerful cancer-fighting carotenoid, while immune-boosting beta-carotene is found in orange and yellow foods.

CHICKEN NUGGETS WITH OVEN-BAKED WEDGES

Unlike the commercial varieties, these chicken nuggets contain 100 percent lean meat, so they are high in protein and low in fat. The potato wedges are also very low in fat as they are baked in the oven instead of being deep fried.

PREPARATION TIME 15 minutes
COOKING TIME 30 minutes

¾ cup whole-wheat flour or wheat germ

1 garlic clove, crushed

2 tablespoons finely grated sharp Cheddar or Parmesan cheese

6 tablespoons water

1 egg white

3 boneless, skinless chicken breasts, about 3½ oz. each, cut into bite-size pieces

sea salt and freshly ground black pepper

Real Tomato Ketchup (page 105), to serve

oven-baked wedges

2 baking potatoes, about 12 oz. in total, cut into wedges

2 tablespoons sunflower oil

a baking tray, lightly greased

serves 4

To make the potato wedges, bring a large saucepan of water to a boil and add the potato pieces. Cook for 10 to 12 minutes until slightly softened, but still firm. Drain well and, when cool enough to handle, dry with paper towels. Transfer the wedges to a roasting pan and drizzle with the oil. Toss carefully so the potatoes are well coated. Sprinkle with a little sea salt. Cook on the top shelf of a preheated oven at 400°F for about 15 minutes, stirring once, until golden brown and crisp.

Meanwhile, put the flour or wheat germ, ½ teaspoon salt, garlic, cheese, and black pepper, to taste, in a shallow dish. Put the water and egg white in a separate bowl and beat lightly. Dip the chicken pieces in the egg white, then roll them in the flour or wheat germ mixture until well coated. Transfer to the prepared baking tray.

Put the baking tray on the middle shelf of the preheated oven and cook the nuggets at the same time as the potato wedges for 10 to 12 minutes, stirring occasionally, until thoroughly cooked.

Serve the nuggets with the oven-baked wedges and some real tomato ketchup.

Did You Know?

Chicken contains all the amino acids that growing bodies need. It also contains vitamin B12, which is needed for the formation of blood and nerve cells.

HOMEMADE SAUSAGES

Children love sausages. However, most version contain poor-quality meat as well as cheap fillers, additives, and lots of salt. This recipe uses 100 percent lean meat and adds flavor in the form of onion, garlic, apples, and herbs.

PREPARATION TIME
15 minutes, plus 30 minutes chilling time
COOKING TIME 15–20 minutes

8 oz. cooking apples, peeled, cored, and grated

10 oz. lean pork, such as loin, finely ground

1 medium onion, finely chopped

1–2 garlic cloves, crushed

2 tablespoons chopped fresh sage leaves

¼ cup whole-wheat flour

2 tablespoons sunflower oil

sea salt and freshly ground black pepper

to serve

lightly steamed seasonal vegetables (optional)

Real Tomato Ketchup (see right)

makes 12

Wrap the grated apple tightly in a clean kitchen towel in order to remove some of the moisture. Put the apple, pork, onion, garlic, and sage in a food processor. Add salt and pepper, to taste, then blend using the pulse button until mixed.

Transfer the mixture to a lightly floured counter. Using damp hands, make 12 small balls about the size of a large apricot. Roll each one into a sausage shape. Put the flour in a shallow dish and dip the sausages into it to coat them evenly. Transfer them to a large plate, cover lightly with plastic wrap, and chill for 30 minutes.

Put the sausages in a nonstick roasting pan and drizzle with a little oil. Cook in a preheated oven at 375°F for 15 to 20 minutes, turning them halfway through. Alternatively, heat the oil in a nonstick skillet, add the sausages, and cook for 12 to 15 minutes over moderate heat, turning frequently, until golden brown and thoroughly cooked.

Serve with lightly steamed seasonal vegetables, if liked, and real tomato ketchup.

VARIATIONS

- To serve, split a warmed whole-wheat pita bread and add a sausage, some shredded lettuce, and tomato slices.
- Freshly ground lean beef or lamb can be used instead of the pork.
- Vary the flavors of the sausages by adding 2 tablespoons chopped fresh mixed herbs or finely grated sharp Cheddar cheese, or 2 to 3 teaspoons mustard or horseradish.

REAL TOMATO KETCHUP

PREPARATION TIME 15 minutes
COOKING TIME 2 hours

3 tablespoons olive oil

2 lb. onions, roughly chopped

3 garlic cloves, crushed

3½ lb. ripe tomatoes, roughly chopped

⅓ cup white wine vinegar

¼–⅓ cup dark brown sugar

½ teaspoon ground cloves

½ teaspoon ground allspice

1 teaspoon mustard seeds

½ teaspoon ground celery seeds

1 teaspoon sea salt

1 teaspoon freshly ground black pepper

makes 5 cups

Heat the oil in large heavy-based saucepan. Add the onions and cook for 8 to 10 minutes, stirring occasionally, until golden brown. Add the garlic and cook for 1 minute. Stir in the tomatoes, vinegar, sugar, cloves, allspice, mustard and celery seeds, and salt and pepper. Bring the mixture to a boil, cover, reduce the heat, and simmer, stirring occasionally, for 1 hour.

Transfer the mixture to a blender or food processor and blend, in batches if necessary, to a fairly smooth puree. Return the puree to the rinsed pan and bring it to a boil. Reduce the heat, cover, and simmer for about 45 minutes, stirring occasionally, until the mixture is thick. Remove the pan from the heat and let cool.

Once cool, pour the tomato sauce into small sterilized jars (page 4) and seal tightly. Store in the refrigerator for up to 1 month. Once opened, use within 1 week.

BURGERS

All kids love burgers. As you can see from these recipes, there is no reason why they should be unhealthy. In fact, they can be a great way of packaging up some really nutritious ingredients. Don't forget to make extra quantities for freezing.

CHICKEN BURGERS

PREPARATION TIME
20 minutes, plus 30 minutes
chilling time
COOKING TIME 12–15 minutes

2 tablespoons olive oil

1 onion, finely chopped

1 celery stalk, finely chopped

1 garlic clove, crushed

2 boneless, skinless chicken
breasts, about 5 oz.
in total, ground

1 large carrot, grated

1 tablespoon finely grated
unwaxed orange zest

1–2 tablespoons chopped
fresh flat-leaf parsley

⅓ cup raisins or dried cranberries

1 egg, beaten

2–3 tablespoons whole-wheat
flour, for coating

sea salt and freshly ground
black pepper

to serve

4 whole-grain rolls

lettuce leaves

4 tomato slices

Real Tomato Ketchup (page 105)

serves 4

Heat the oil in a skillet, add the onion, celery, and garlic, and sauté for 5 minutes until soft. Transfer the mixture to a large bowl and add the chicken, carrot, orange zest, parsley, raisins or cranberries, and egg. Season to taste with salt and pepper and mix well.

Using damp hands, shape the mixture into 4 burgers. Put the flour in a shallow dish, dip the burgers in it to coat them evenly. Transfer them to a plate, cover lightly with plastic wrap, and chill for 30 minutes.

Heat a nonstick skillet, add the burgers, and dry fry over medium heat for 5 to 6 minutes until golden underneath. Turn the burgers over and cook for 5 to 6 minutes on the other side until golden and thoroughly cooked.

To serve, put a burger in a whole-grain roll, top with crisp lettuce leaves, a slice of tomato, and a little homemade tomato ketchup.

COOK'S TIP
- After being shaped, the burgers can be wrapped and frozen for up to 1 month.

BEEF BURGERS

PREPARATION TIME 8–10 minutes,
plus 30 minutes chilling time
COOKING TIME 15–20 minutes

12 oz. extra lean ground beef

1 small onion, finely chopped

1 small zucchini, grated

1 tablespoon chopped fresh flat-leaf parsley
or fresh sage leaves

freshly ground black pepper

lightly steamed seasonal vegetables, to serve

a baking tray

makes 8

Put all the ingredients in a large bowl and mix with your hands until they come together to form a large ball. Shape the mixture into 8 balls and flatten them into burgers. Transfer to a large plate, lightly cover with plastic wrap, and chill for 30 minutes.

Put the burgers on a nonstick baking tray and cook in a preheated oven at 375°F for 15 to 20 minutes until thoroughly cooked. Alternatively, cook under a preheated hot broiler for 4 to 6 minutes on each side, or dry fry in a hot, nonstick skillet for 3 to 4 minutes on each side.

Serve with your choice of steamed vegetables.

COOK'S TIP
- After being shaped, the burgers can be wrapped and frozen for up to 1 month.

NUT BURGERS

PREPARATION TIME
20 minutes, plus 30 minutes
chilling time
COOKING TIME 30 minutes

8 oz. mixed unsalted nuts, such
as cashews, walnuts, and peanuts

2 tablespoons olive oil

1 onion, very finely chopped

2 garlic cloves, crushed

3 oz. button mushrooms, wiped
and finely chopped

1 small yellow bell pepper,
seeded and finely chopped

1 cup fresh whole-wheat
bread crumbs

1 medium carrot, grated

1 tablespoon chopped
fresh parsley

2–3 fresh sage leaves,
finely chopped

1 egg, beaten

whole-wheat flour, for coating

sea salt and freshly ground
black pepper

to serve

4 whole-grain rolls

lettuce leaves

4 tomato slices

Real Tomato Ketchup (page 105)

a baking tray, lightly greased

serves 4–6

Put the nuts in a food processor and blend until finely chopped.

Heat 1 tablespoon of the oil in a heavy-based saucepan, add the onion and garlic, and sauté gently, stirring occasionally, for 5 minutes or until soft and golden. Add the mushrooms and pepper and cook for 3 minutes more. Remove the pan from the heat and mix in all the remaining ingredients except the flour and the remaining oil.

Using your hands, bring the mixture together to form a large ball, adding a little water if the mixture is too dry. Shape the mixture into 4 burgers. Put the flour in a shallow dish, dip the burgers in it to coat them evenly. Transfer to a plate, lightly cover with plastic wrap, and chill for 30 minutes.

Put the burgers on the prepared baking tray and brush lightly with the remaining oil. Bake in a preheated oven at 375°F for 20 minutes until golden and piping hot. To serve, put a burger in a whole-grain roll, top with crisp lettuce leaves, a slice of tomato, and a little homemade tomato ketchup.

VEGETABLE BURGERS

PREPARATION TIME 20 minutes,
plus 30 minutes chilling time
COOKING TIME 25–30 minutes

2–3 tablespoons sunflower oil

1 red onion, finely chopped

2 garlic cloves, crushed

3½ oz. mushrooms, wiped and finely chopped

⅔ cup unsalted cashew nuts, finely chopped

1 cup cooked brown rice

5 oz. carrots, grated

½ cup cooked peas

½ cup cooked corn kernels

½ cup fresh whole-wheat bread crumbs

1 tablespoon chopped fresh parsley

5–6 tablespoons whole-wheat flour

sea salt and freshly ground black pepper

a baking tray, lightly greased

serves 6

Heat 1 tablespoon of the oil in a saucepan. Add the onion and garlic, and sauté, stirring occasionally, for 5 minutes or until soft. Add the mushrooms and continue to cook, stirring occasionally, for 5 minutes more until the vegetables are lightly cooked and golden.

Remove the pan from the heat and stir in the nuts, rice, carrots, peas, corn kernels, bread crumbs, parsley, 1–2 tablespoons flour, and salt and pepper, to taste. Using damp hands, shape the mixture into 6 burgers, then coat them evenly in the remaining flour. Transfer to a plate, lightly cover with plastic wrap, and chill for 30 minutes.

Put the burgers on the prepared baking tray and brush lightly with the remaining oil. Bake in a preheated oven at 350°F for 15 to 20 minutes until crisp and piping hot. Alternatively, cook under a preheated hot broiler for 10 to 12 minutes, turning the burgers halfway through. Serve immediately.

MINI SHEPHERD'S PIES WITH FOUR VEG MASH

This recipe takes a little longer than most of the others to make, but you will have 8 mini pies that can be popped in the freezer and pulled out on those days when you don't have time to cook. There are 11 different vegetables in this dish—a real health booster.

PREPARATION TIME 25–30 minutes
COOKING TIME about 45 minutes

1 tablespoon olive oil

6 oz. leeks, thinly sliced

1½ lb. extra-lean ground lamb

2 medium onions, finely chopped

2 celery stalks, finely chopped

1½ tablespoons whole-wheat flour

½ tablespoon Worcestershire sauce

1 cup organic vegetable broth

1 lb. ripe tomatoes, chopped

1 red bell pepper, seeded and chopped

2 carrots, grated

2 cups frozen peas

¾ cup grated Cheddar cheese

vegetable mash

6 oz. potatoes, chopped into small chunks

8 oz. sweet potatoes, chopped into small chunks

5 oz. carrots, chopped into small chunks

6 oz. parsnips, chopped into small chunks

freshly grated nutmeg, to taste

1–2 tablespoons milk

sea salt and freshly ground black pepper

8 individual ovenproof dishes, 1½ cups each

makes 8 small pies

To make the vegetable mash, bring a large saucepan of water to a boil, add the potatoes, sweet potatoes, carrots, and parsnips and cook for about 15 minutes until the vegetables are soft. Drain, return to the pan, and mash. Add nutmeg, salt, and pepper to taste, and enough milk to give a soft but not runny mixture. Set aside.

Heat the oil in a nonstick skillet, add the leeks, and sauté for 5 to 8 minutes or until soft. Remove the leeks with a slotted spoon and set aside.

Wipe the skillet with paper towels, then return it to the heat. Add the ground lamb and dry fry for 5 to 8 minutes, stirring frequently, until sealed. Add the onions and celery and fry for a further 5 minutes. Drain through a colander to remove any fat, then return to the rinsed skillet. Sprinkle in the flour and the Worcestershire sauce and cook, stirring, for 2 minutes. Slowly stir in the broth, tomatoes, pepper, carrots, and peas. Bring to a boil, reduce the heat, and simmer for 10 to 15 minutes until most of the excess liquid has been absorbed and the sauce is thick.

Spoon the meat mixture into the ovenproof dishes and top with a layer of the leeks. Spoon over the vegetable mash to cover the filling, then sprinkle with the grated cheese.

Cook under a preheated broiler for 10 to 15 minutes until the tops are golden brown and bubbling. Alternatively, cook in a preheated oven at 375°F for 20 to 25 minutes. Serve hot.

COOK'S TIP

- To freeze, prepare the pies and let cool completely. Wrap and label, then freeze for up to 1 month. Defrost thoroughly, then cook in a preheated oven at 375°F for 20 to 25 minutes until piping hot.

VEGETABLES

It's a myth that kids won't eat vegetables. Dip asparagus spears in hot, melted garlic butter, add some chopped dry-cured bacon to peas, or drizzle a little honey over baby carrots and watch those vegetables disappear! Here are a few more ideas.

BROCCOLI CHEESE

PREPARATION TIME 15–20 minutes
COOKING TIME 18–25 minutes

1 lb. broccoli, divided into bite-size florets

cheese sauce

¼ cup sunflower oil

¼ cup flour

1¾ cups milk

¾ cups grated sharp Cheddar cheese, plus extra for sprinkling

an ovenproof dish

serves 4

Steam the broccoli over gently simmering water for 8 minutes or until it is tender but still has some bite. Drain and transfer to an ovenproof dish.

To make the cheese sauce, heat the oil in a small saucepan, and stir in the flour. Cook, stirring, for 2 minutes. Remove the pan from the heat and gradually stir in the milk. Return the pan to the heat and cook, stirring continuously, until the sauce thickens.

Add the grated cheese to the sauce and stir until it has melted. Pour the sauce over the broccoli and sprinkle with a little more grated cheese. Cook under a preheated moderate broiler for 10 to 15 minutes until the cheese is golden brown and bubbling. Serve.

SESAME SUGARSNAP PEAS

PREPARATION TIME 4 minutes
COOKING TIME 4–5 minutes

1 tablespoon sunflower oil

1 lb. sugarsnap peas

2 teaspoons sesame seeds

2 teaspoons sesame oil

serves 4

Heat a wok until hot, then add the sunflower oil. When the oil is hot, add the sugarsnap peas. Stir fry for about 4 minutes, stirring continuously, until tender. Add the sesame seeds and oil, and stir fry for 1 minute more. Serve immediately.

CREAMY SPINACH

PREPARATION TIME 5 minutes
COOKING TIME 3–4 minutes

1 lb. fresh spinach

2 tablespoons cream

freshly grated nutmeg (optional)

serves 4

Discard any hard central stalks from the spinach and wash the leaves thoroughly in plenty of cold water. Drain well, then put the spinach in a large saucepan with only the water left clinging to the leaves. Cook for 2 to 3 minutes until wilted. Drain well, squeezing out any excess water, then chop.

Return the spinach to the rinsed pan and add 1 teaspoon water and the cream. Heat over medium heat for 1 minute, stirring. Serve immediately, sprinkled with a little freshly grated nutmeg, if using.

SHREDDED CABBAGE & HAM

PREPARATION TIME 5 minutes
COOKING TIME 6–7 minutes

1 lb. cabbage, such as Savoy, shredded

2 tablespoons cream

2 thick slices of honey-roasted ham, fat discarded, roughly chopped into small pieces

sea salt and freshly ground black pepper

serves 4

Put the cabbage in a large saucepan of boiling water and return to a boil. Cover, reduce the heat, and simmer gently for 4 to 5 minutes until tender. Drain well.

Return the cabbage to the warm pan and stir in the cream, ham, and salt and pepper, to taste. Heat gently, stirring, for 2 minutes until hot. Serve immediately.

DESSERTS

Desserts offer a great opportunity to encourage children to eat more fruit. However, they can also fill them with lots of sugar, fat, and additives they don't need. The nutritional content of some of the popular, commercially prepared desserts doesn't make happy reading.

CUSTARD Made in the traditional way—with eggs, milk, and sugar—custard is a great source of protein, calcium, vitamins, and minerals. However, many commercial varieties contain large amounts of sugar and additives, and some "just-add-water" powdered versions even manage to bypass any nutritional benefits that may be had from adding fresh milk.

JELL-O is a highly synthetic mixture consisting of little more than sugar, artificial colorings and flavorings, and generous amounts of gelatin.

ICE CREAM As is often the case, the more expensive varieties tend to contain better quality ingredients. However, most storebought ice cream is a world away from the traditional recipe of milk, cream, sugar, and eggs (page 117). Most contain a lot of fat and sugar and are bulked out with air and water. Production costs are kept to a minimum by using artificial colorings and flavorings, milk powders, emulsifiers, and hardened vegetable fats.

MOUSSES Supermarkets now stock a vast array of mousse-like desserts. Most are little more than a blend of synthetic ingredients, such as emulsifiers, artificial colorings, flavorings, and preservatives, and large amounts of sugar. The "fruit" varieties contain very little, if any, fruit and most offer few or no nutritional benefits.

YOGURT Plain yogurt is a naturally healthy food that can be a good source of calcium, protein, and vitamins. Those that are flavored with natural fruit purees are also great choices. However, the potential health benefits of many yogurts, especially those marketed specifically at children, are often outweighed by the high quantities of added sugar (some small pots contain as much as 4 teaspoons) or sweeteners, flavorings, and additives. Many cheaper yogurts contain no fruit at all, only chemical fruit flavors. Those that do contain fruit invariably contain artificial preservatives, too.

SERVING DESSERT

Children don't need dessert every day. It's far better to encourage them to get into the habit of heading for the fruit bowl if they want something sweet after dinner. Not serving dessert on a daily basis also helps to avoid the common scenario of the entrée being pushed aside in anticipation of something sweeter to come. Avoid the temptation to use dessert as a bribe to get your children to eat their entrée, because this will only serve to reinforce in their mind that savory foods are to be endured and make sweet, fatty foods even more irresistible.

However, if you do serve a dessert, steer clear of commercially prepared ones as much as possible. In this chapter you'll find lots of fruit-packed ideas that are totally additive-free and contain only the necessary amounts of sugar and fat. If you buy a ready-made dessert, check the label for the sugar content per 100 g: more than 10 g is high, less than 2 g is low.

REAL ALTERNATIVES
sprinkle bite-size chunks of melon with a little grated nutmeg • cut a banana in half lengthwise, put some chopped chocolate in the middle, and heat for a few seconds in the microwave until the chocolate has melted • fresh fruit salad served with some sour cream or Homemade Custard (page 126) • sliced mango served with fresh raspberries • fresh or frozen strawberries blended with Homemade Custard (page 126) • frozen summer fruits blended with low-fat natural fromage frais and a little honey • fruit kabobs, broiled and drizzled with a little honey • Greek or plain yogurt sweetened with honey and sprinkled with some Granola (page 32), finely chopped nuts, or seeds to add extra crunch • fruit compote, either commercially prepared with no added sugar or homemade (page 121), topped with Granola (page 32), and a small scoop of homemade Vanilla Ice Cream (page 117) • chunks of low-fat Cheddar cheese and apple on toothpicks • blend together a banana with some Homemade Custard (page 126), add a dessert spoon of grated chocolate (at least 70 percent cocoa solids), and heat in the microwave on HIGH for about 1 minute until the chocolate has melted

VANILLA ICE CREAM

All kids love ice cream. However, all but the most expensive storebought versions are little more than a cheap blend of artificial colorings and flavorings, milk powders, emulsifiers, sugars, and hardened vegetable fats. This recipe is made in the old-fashioned way, using nothing but eggs, milk, sugar, and cream. If you follow the variations, you can pack in a whole load of fruit too!

PREPARATION TIME 25 minutes
COOKING TIME 12 15 minutes
FREEZING TIME 3 hours

1 recipe Homemade Custard (page 126)

1¼ cups heavy cream

superfine sugar, to taste

an ice cream maker (optional)

serves 6–8

Set the freezer to rapid freeze, or if using an ice cream maker, put the bowl in the freezer the night before.

Make the custard, cover with a piece of damp wax paper, and let cool. Whip the cream until soft peaks form, then stir it into the cooled custard. Taste and add a little sugar, if necessary.

Pour the mixture into a freezerproof container and freeze for 1 hour. Remove from the freezer and stir, breaking up any ice crystals that have formed. Return it to the freezer for a further 2 hours, stirring at least twice. Leave for a further 1 hour or until frozen.

If using an ice cream maker, pour the mixture into the machine and churn for 35 to 45 minutes or until softly frozen. Transfer to a freezerproof container, cover, and label.

When ready to serve, transfer the ice cream to the refrigerator for at least 30 minutes to soften slightly. Serve in scoops.

The ice cream can be stored in the freezer for up to 1 month.

VARIATIONS

- **Fruit Ice Cream** Simmer 10 oz. ripe fruit (such as mango, raspberries, strawberries, papaya, or mixed summer berries) with ¼ cup water and 1 to 2 tablespoons superfine sugar for 5 minutes or until the fruit has collapsed. Let cool, transfer to a blender, and process to form a puree. Add the puree to the creamy custard mixture and continue as in the main recipe. Crushed ripe fruit can be added as well for added flavor.
- **Raspberry Ripple Ice Cream** Stir ⅔ cup raspberry puree (prepare as directed in Fruit Ice Cream, above) through the semi-frozen vanilla ice cream, giving a rippled effect. Do not stir the ice cream again after adding the puree.
- **Chocolate Ice Cream** Put 2½ oz. finely chopped semisweet chocolate (at least 70 percent cocoa solids) in a large heatproof bowl. Pour the hot custard onto the chocolate and stir until smooth. Cover and let cool, then continue as in the main recipe.
- Other ingredients can be folded into the ice cream before it is frozen. Try adding chopped nuts, chopped chocolate, or chopped dried fruit, such as raisins, apricots, or cherries.

STICKY TOFFEE & APRICOT SAUCE

PREPARATION TIME 5–8 minutes
COOKING TIME 15–18 minutes

1 cup dried apricots, roughly chopped

2 tablespoons light brown sugar

1 tablespoon butter

makes 1¼ cups

Put the apricots, sugar, and ¾ cup water in a heavy-based saucepan. Bring to a boil, then cover and reduce the heat. Simmer for 12 to 15 minutes or until the apricots are really soft. Let cool, then transfer to a blender and process to form a puree. Return the puree to the rinsed pan, add the butter, and heat gently until the butter has melted. Stir, then serve poured over ice cream.

STRAWBERRY SAUCE

PREPARATION TIME 5–8 minutes
COOKING TIME 10 minutes

2 pints strawberries, hulled

2–4 tablespoons superfine sugar (depending on the ripeness of the strawberries)

2 tablespoons freshly squeezed lemon juice

makes 1 quart

Cut any large strawberries in half, then put them in a heavy-based saucepan. Add the sugar, to taste, lemon juice, and ⅔ cup water. Heat gently, stirring occasionally, until the sugar has dissolved.

Bring to a boil, reduce the heat, and simmer for 5 minutes or until the strawberries are really soft.

Transfer to a blender and process to form a smooth sauce. Pour over ice cream, to serve.

VARIATION

• Other berries can be used in place of the strawberries. Try raspberries, blackberries, blueberries, or a mixture. Plums, greengages, or ripe mangoes can also be used.

KNICKERBOCKER GLORY

No childhood would be complete without the experience of eating a knickerbocker glory. These are packed full of fruit and made from homemade, additive-free ice cream, which is high in both vitamin C and calcium.

PREPARATION TIME
10–15 minutes

2½ pints raspberries

½ recipe Chocolate Ice Cream (page 117)

10 oz. plain yogurt

1 pint strawberries, cut in half if large

½ recipe Vanilla Ice Cream (page 117)

2 oz. semisweet chocolate (at least 70 percent cocoa solids), roughly chopped or grated

4 tall sundae glasses

serves 4

Put 1 tablespoon raspberries in the bottom of each glass and top with 1 scoop of chocolate ice cream. Spoon over the yogurt, then top with the strawberries, reserving 4 of the strawberries, to decorate.

Add 1 scoop of vanilla ice cream, then scatter over a little chopped chocolate. Add 1 more tablespoon of raspberries to each glass, then finish with 1 scoop of vanilla or chocolate ice cream. Sprinkle with a little more chopped chocolate, top with a strawberry, and serve immediately.

Did You Know?

Strawberries contain more vitamin C than any other berry. Just one-quarter of the strawberries used here provides more than twice the amount a child needs in a day.

FRUIT COMPOTES

Stirred into yogurt, ice cream, and custard, blended into smoothies or eaten just as they are, fruit compotes are extremely versatile. Make double the quantity and freeze what you don't want to use immediately in small plastic containers. The compote can then be defrosted in the microwave at a moment's notice.

RHUBARB COMPOTE

PREPARATION TIME
5–8 minutes
COOKING TIME 15 minutes

2 tablespoons ginger ale

¼ cup superfine sugar

1 lb. rhubarb, cut into
small pieces

plain yogurt, to serve (optional)

serves 4

Put the ginger ale, sugar, and 3 tablespoons water in a large saucepan. Heat gently, stirring until the sugar has dissolved, then simmer for 2 minutes.

Add the rhubarb and poach it in the ginger syrup for about 10 minutes or until the fruit is tender. Remove from the heat and let cool before serving. If liked, stir a few tablespoons of the compote through some plain yogurt, to serve.

COOK'S TIP
• Cooking the rhubarb in ginger ale helps to remove some of the tartness of the rhubarb. The cooking time will vary according to which type of rhubarb is used.

VARIATION
• **Rhubarb Fool** Cook the rhubarb as above, then drain off any excess cooking syrup. Transfer the rhubarb to a blender and process briefly. Stir into Homemade Custard (page 126), let cool, and serve.

Did You Know?
Rhubarb is a good source of magnesium, which works with calcium to promote healthy bones, release energy, and absorb other nutrients.

CHERRY COMPOTE

PREPARATION TIME
15 minutes
COOKING TIME 20 minutes

1 lb. unblemished cherries

¼ cup superfine sugar

serves 4

Pit the cherries. Do this over a bowl so you can catch any juice.

Put the cherries and any juice in a heavy-based saucepan. Add the sugar and simmer gently, stirring occasionally, until the sugar has dissolved. Simmer for another 5 to 8 minutes or until the fruit is tender. Using a slotted draining spoon, remove the cherries from the liquid and transfer them to a serving bowl.

Bring the cooking liquor to a boil, then simmer gently for 8 to 10 minutes or until reduced and slightly syrupy. Pour the sauce over the cherries and serve.

CHOCOLATE MOUSSE

Chocolate with a high cocoa solid content (at least 70 percent) is a good source of antioxidants. It also contains iron and magnesium.

PREPARATION TIME 5–8 minutes, plus 1 hour chilling time

3½ oz. semisweet chocolate (at least 70 percent cocoa solids)

4 eggs, separated

1 teaspoon unsweetened cocoa powder

4 individual dishes or glasses, 5 oz. each

serves 4

Break the chocolate into small pieces and put them in a heatproof bowl. Place the bowl over a saucepan of gently simmering, not boiling, water (make sure the bottom of the bowl doesn't touch the water). Heat gently until melted. Remove the bowl from the heat and stir until smooth. Let cool.

Beat the eggs yolks into the cooled chocolate one at a time, beating well after each addition. Put the egg whites in a clean, grease-free bowl and beat with a hand-held electric beater until stiff peaks form. Using a large metal spoon, gently stir the egg whites into the chocolate mixture, taking care not to overmix and knock out the air.

Spoon the mixture into 4 individual dishes or glasses, then chill in the refrigerator for 1 hour. Sprinkle with a little cocoa powder and serve.

RASPBERRY MOUSSE

Not only is this mousse utterly delicious, it is packed with raspberries which are rich in vitamin C and are higher in folic acid and zinc than most other fruit.

PREPARATION TIME 12–15 minutes, plus 1 hour chilling time
COOKING TIME 10 minutes

1 pint raspberries, plus extra to serve

¼ cup freshly squeezed orange juice

about ¼ cup superfine sugar

1¼ cups heavy cream

2 egg whites

2 squares semisweet chocolate (at least 70 percent cocoa solids), grated, to serve

4 individual dishes or glasses, 1 cup each

serves 4

Put the raspberries, orange juice, and sugar, to taste, in a heavy-based saucepan. Simmer gently for 10 minutes, stirring occasionally, until the fruit has collapsed and softened. Let cool slightly, then transfer to a blender and process to form a puree. If you would like a smooth result, push the puree through a fine non-metallic strainer. Let cool.

Beat the cream until soft peaks form, then stir in the cooled raspberry puree. Put the egg whites in a clean, grease-free bowl and beat with a hand-held electric beater until stiff peaks form. Using a large metal spoon, gently stir the egg whites into the raspberry mixture, taking care not to overmix and knock out the air.

Spoon the mousse into 4 individual dishes or glasses. Cover and chill in the refrigerator for at least 1 hour. Serve topped with extra raspberries and some grated chocolate.

COOK'S TIP
- You can omit the whisked egg whites from this recipe if you are serving it to somebody who should avoid uncooked eggs (page 4).

MARITIME MANGOES

One serving of this dessert contains one orange and half a mango, so it's packed with vitamin C to keep the immune system healthy.

PREPARATION TIME
15 minutes
FREEZING TIME 3 hours,
plus 30 minutes softening time

4 large oranges

2 ripe mangoes

2 tablespoons finely grated
unwaxed orange zest

3 tablespoons low-fat
plain yogurt

3 tablespoons sour cream

2 squares semisweet chocolate
(at least 70 percent cocoa solids),
grated, to serve (optional)

serves 4

Set the freezer to rapid freeze. Cut the oranges in half, scooping out the flesh and pith, taking care to leave the orange shells intact. If necessary, cut a small slice from the base of each orange shell to ensure they can stand upright.

Peel the mangoes and cut the flesh away from the stones. Chop the flesh into small pieces. Put the mango and orange flesh, orange zest, yogurt, and sour cream in a blender and process for 2 to 3 minutes until smooth.

Pour the mixture into a freezerproof container and freeze for 2 hours, stirring occasionally, to break up any ice crystals. Spoon the mixture into the orange shells, then freeze for 1 hour or until solid. Transfer the oranges to the refrigerator 30 minutes before serving to soften slightly. Top each one with a little grated chocolate, if using, and serve.

STRAWBERRY MOUNTAIN

Strawberries are a great source of vitamin C and this dessert is so packed with them that it contains almost twice the recommended daily amount of vitamin C a child needs in a day.

PREPARATION TIME
10–15 minutes
FREEZING TIME 1½–2 hours

4 pints strawberries, hulled

¾ cup confectioners' sugar,
plus 1 tablespoon extra

freshly squeezed juice of
2 lemons

2 tablespoons heavy cream

serves 6–8

Put the strawberries in a blender or food processor and blend to form a puree. If you want a smoother result, push the puree through a non-metallic strainer to remove the pips. Transfer to a bowl and beat in the sugar and lemon juice. Pour into a shallow, freezerproof container and freeze for 1½ to 2 hours until solid.

Meanwhile, put the cream and 1 tablespoon confectioners' sugar in a small bowl and mix well. Cover and refrigerate.

Transfer the frozen strawberry mixture to the refrigerator 30 minutes before serving. When ready to serve, use a strong fork to scrape shreds of the frozen strawberries and divide them between 6 or 8 serving dishes. Top each serving with 1 teaspoon of the chilled cream and serve immediately.

COOK'S TIP
- Use a shallow, freezerproof container no more than 2 inches deep so that the mixture freezes quickly.

VARIATION
- Replace the strawberries with raspberries, firm melons, plums, or oranges.

OATY APPLE CRUNCH

This crunch is packed with apples, oats, and nuts, which all release their sugars slowly into the blood stream making it a real energy booster.

PREPARATION TIME 15 minutes
COOKING TIME 20–30 minutes

1½ lb. cooking apples, peeled, cored, and sliced

1 teaspoon ground cinnamon

3 tablespoons light brown sugar

Homemade Custard (see below), to serve

oat topping

1¼ cups old-fashioned rolled oats

1 tablespoon wheat germ

2 oz. nuts, such as pecans, hazelnuts, almonds, and walnuts, chopped or flaked

2 tablespoons sunflower seeds

2 tablespoons sesame seeds

2 tablespoons honey

2 tablespoons sunflower oil

a baking tray

an ovenproof dish, 6 cup capacity

serves 4–6

To make the oat topping, put the oats, wheat germ, nuts, and seeds in a heatproof bowl and mix well. Heat the honey and oil in a small saucepan over medium heat, stirring, until blended. Pour the honey mixture over the oats and stir until well coated. Spoon the mixture onto a baking tray and bake in a preheated oven at 350°F for 10 to 15 minutes or until the mixture is lightly toasted. Remove from the oven and let cool. (Once cold, the oat mixture can be store in an airtight container for up to 1 week).

Meanwhile, put the apples, cinnamon, sugar, and ¼ cup water in a saucepan. Cover and heat gently, stirring occasionally, for 10 to 15 minutes until the apples have softened and the sugar has dissolved.

Transfer the apples to the ovenproof dish, sprinkle with the toasted oat mixture, and press down lightly. Increase the oven temperature to 400°F and bake in the oven for 10 to 15 minutes until bubbling. Serve with homemade custard.

COOK'S TIP
- Other fruits can be used instead of the apples. Try fresh apricots or plums, apples and blackberries, or frozen summer berries, defrosted.

HOMEMADE CUSTARD

This mouthwatering custard takes only minutes to make and is free from the artificial thickeners, colorings, preservatives, and sweeteners found in commercial versions.

PREPARATION TIME 5 minutes, plus 15 minutes infusing time
COOKING TIME 12–15 minutes

1½ cups heavy cream

2½ cups whole milk

1 vanilla bean

3 eggs

2 tablespoons superfine sugar

makes 2¾ cups

Pour the cream and milk into a heavy-based saucepan and add the vanilla bean. Heat gently until it reaches just below boiling point. Remove the pan from the heat, cover, and let infuse for 15 minutes.

Beat the eggs and sugar together, then gradually add the infused cream and milk, beating constantly. Strain the mixture into a clean saucepan. Heat gently, beating constantly, until the custard starts to thicken. Remove the pan from the heat and continue to beat until the custard cools slightly and thickens. Pour into a heatproof pitcher and serve immediately.

VARIATIONS
- **Strawberry Custard** Blend 1 cup ripe, hulled strawberries to a puree, then stir into the prepared custard, adding extra sugar, to taste, if necessary.
- **Banana Custard** Stir 1 to 2 ripe mashed bananas into the prepared custard.
- **Chocolate Custard** Stir 3½ oz. melted semisweet chocolate (at least 70 percent cocoa solids) into the prepared custard.

MIXED BERRY TARTLETS

If you haven't got time to make the pastry yourself, just buy a large, ready-made pie crust and fill it with the crème fraîche or sour cream and fruit.

PREPARATION TIME 20–25 minutes,
plus 30 minutes chilling time
COOKING TIME 17 minutes

¾ cup white flour, plus extra for dusting

¾ cup whole-wheat flour

6½ tablespoons unsalted butter, chilled and
cut into small pieces

1 tablespoon finely grated unwaxed orange zest

for the filling

2 pints mixed summer berries, including blueberries,
strawberries, and raspberries

1¼ cups crème fraîche or thick yogurt

1 tablespoon finely grated unwaxed orange zest

2 teaspoons confectioners' sugar

a cookie cutter, 3 inches diameter

small tartlet pans

makes 12

To make the pastry, put the flours, butter and orange zest in a food processor and blend for 1 to 2 minutes until the mixture resembles bread crumbs. With the machine running, gradually pour 3 to 4 tablespoons cold water through the feed tube until the mixture forms a ball.

Transfer the dough to a lightly floured counter and knead it until smooth and pliable. Wrap and chill in the refrigerator for 30 minutes.

Roll out the pastry thinly on a lightly floured counter. Using the cookie cutter, cut out 12 rounds and line the tartlet pans with them. Prick the bases lightly with a fork, then put a small piece of crumbled foil in each one.

Bake in a preheated oven at 400°F for 12 minutes. Remove the foil and return the pastry cases to the oven for another 3 to 5 minutes until the pastry is cooked. Remove from the oven and let cool before filling.

To prepare the filling, hull the strawberries and raspberries, if necessary, and cut any large fruit in half. Put the crème fraîche or yogurt and orange zest in a bowl and mix. Spoon it into the tartlet crusts and put the fruit on top. Sprinkle with a little confectioners' sugar and serve immediately.

COOK'S TIP

- To save time, you can make double the amount of pastry given here and wrap, label, and freeze the extra quantity. Use within 1 month. Defrost thoroughly in the refrigerator before using.

Did You Know?

Berries are nature's powerhouse fruit. They taste great and are densely packed with antioxidants, phytochemicals, and flavonoids. They are also high in fiber and vitamin C, and relatively low in sugar. Blueberries contain more antioxidants than other fruit so don't just add them to desserts, add them to yogurt, breakfast cereals, or eat them just as they are!

PARTY FOOD

Why is it that when it comes to birthdays, we parents think it is perfectly acceptable to feed our children—and all their friends—obscene amounts of sugar, fat, and salt along with a cocktail of artificial colorings, flavorings, and preservatives?

Synthetic, sugar-laden sodas, potato chips, and snacks packed with saturated fat and salt, cheap white bread sandwiches filled with high fat fillings, sausages made from the cheapest offcuts of meat, and commercially prepared birthday cakes decorated with sometimes as many as five separate colorings (many of which have been shown to cause behavioral problems in up to 25 percent of all small children) have all come to be accepted as normal birthday party fare. Given that most children experience huge sugar rushes after eating these foods, it's no wonder that most children's parties have a tendency to disintegrate into utter chaos.

However, the good news is that it's perfectly simple to create birthday party feasts that your children will genuinely love and that are good for them. In this chapter you'll find a collection of recipes designed to inspire you to prepare a really healthy (and delicious) celebratory feast, many of which can be used at any time, not just for parties. Equally, there are lots of ideas throughout the rest of the book that would make a welcome party-time treat (see list, far right).

DRINKS

Commercially prepared sodas are very high in sugar and additives. So instead, serve sparkling mineral water mixed with fresh fruit juice or a little low-sugar fruit syrup. For lots more healthy drink ideas, see pages 42, 68, and 71.

PARTY BAGS

If you want to provide a party bag for each child to take home, avoid filling them with sugar- and additive-laden candy. Instead, choose non-food items like stickers, mini crayons, balloons, or bubble blowing kits.

REAL ALTERNATIVES
Honey-glazed top-quality, high meat content organic sausages on toothpicks • cherry tomatoes and cheese cubes on toothpicks • fruit platter, including grapes, melon slices, strawberries, clementines, and kiwi fruit • chocolate crunchies—whole bran cereal and raisins stirred into melted chocolate and served in paper cake cups • any of the sandwich suggestions from page 55, cut into small pieces or shaped with a cookie cutter • bowls of dried fruit, such as cherries, raisins, and apricots • English digestive biscuits topped with cream cheese and halved grapes • hot dogs made from top-quality, high meat content organic sausages, served in whole-grain rolls with fresh Salsa (page 96) or Real Tomato Ketchup (page 105) • thick slices of organic ham spread with cream cheese, rolled up and secured with a toothpick

PRESENTATION

Children are even more easily swayed by the look of food than adults. Therefore, the key to ensuring your healthy, wholesome spread is met with as much enthusiasm as the usual array of junk food that is on offer at parties is to focus on presentation. Cut sandwiches into fun shapes using cookie cutters; make faces on mini pizzas using vegetables; chop up brightly colored fruit and arrange it on the table; pile the hazelnut brownies into a pyramid; and make best use of all the usual themed tablecloths, paper plates, hats, and streamers.

PARTY FOOD IDEAS FROM THE REST OF THE BOOK
Apricot and Walnut Bars (page 60) cut into bite-size pieces • Double Chocolate and Hazelnut Brownies (page 64) cut into bite-size squares • Gingerbread People (page 63) • Vanilla Ice Cream (page 117)—why not create a homemade ice cream parlor with different flavored ice creams and lots of different toppings and sauces? • a selection of dips (pages 48–51) served with toasted whole-wheat pita bread strips, Bread Sticks (page 48), crunchy Vegetable Sticks, and Roasted Root Dippers (page 51) • Coleslaw (page 59) • Tuna Pasta Salad (page 56) • Couscous Salad (page 56) • Oaty Chocolate Crunchies (page 60) • Sweet Potato Fries (page 90) • Oven-baked Wedges (page 102) • Vegetable Chips (page 46) • Homemade Sausages with Real Tomato Ketchup (page 105)

SMOKED SALMON TORTILLA WHEELS

Over recent years, the excessive use of chemicals, antibiotics, artificial colorings, and growth promoters in farmed salmon has given rise to a variety of health concerns. Where possible, buy wild or organically farmed salmon

PREPARATION TIME
15 minutes

4 small flour tortillas

¼ cup low-fat cream cheese

1 teaspoon finely grated unwaxed lemon zest

1 tablespoon freshly snipped chives

7 oz. thinly sliced smoked salmon

1 tablespoon freshly squeezed lemon juice

freshly ground black pepper (optional)

to serve (optional)

cherry tomatoes

lettuce leaves

lemon wedges

toothpicks

makes 32

Wrap the tortillas in foil and heat in a preheated oven at 350°F for 10 minutes, or according to the instructions on the packet. Let cool.

Meanwhile, put the cream cheese, lemon zest, and chives in a bowl and beat with a wooden spoon until softened.

Spread 1 tablespoon of the cream cheese mixture over each tortilla and top with some thinly sliced smoked salmon. Sprinkle with a little lemon juice and grind over some black pepper, if using. Roll up tightly and secure with toothpicks. If not using immediately, wrap in damp wax paper and store in the refrigerator for up to 3 hours until required.

To serve, cut into small slices and discard the toothpicks. Arrange the tortilla wheels on a serving plate and put some cherry tomatoes, lettuce leaves, and lemon wedges, if using, around the plate.

COOK'S TIP

* The tortilla wheels can be frozen before cutting into slices as long as the salmon hasn't been previously frozen. Wrap well, label, and freeze for up to 1 month. To serve, defrost thoroughly in the refrigerator, then cut into thin slices.

VARIATIONS

* Replace the cream cheese and smoked salmon with Smoked Trout Pâté (page 52).
* Use cream cheese mixed with a small amount of tomato paste and some thinly sliced ham.
* Spread Guacamole (page 51) over the tortillas and top with thin strips of red and yellow bell peppers or blanched baby asparagus spears. Roll up and secure as above. Leave in the refrigerator for at least 15 minutes before cutting into wheels.

Did You Know?

This recipe can be made using whole-wheat bread instead of tortillas, but tortillas have a much lower rating on the glycemic index (approximately half that of whole-wheat bread), so they provide a far steadier, more sustained rise in blood sugar levels.

HONEY-GLAZED CHICKEN DRUMSTICKS

What could be more nutritious, simple or delicious than these honey-glazed chicken drumsticks?

PREPARATION TIME
5 minutes
COOKING TIME 25 minutes

12 small chicken drumsticks, about 3 oz. each

6 tablespoons honey

serves 4

Lightly rinse the chicken drumsticks, removing the skin, if preferred. Put them in a roasting pan with 4 tablespoons water. Bake in a preheated oven at 375°F for 5 minutes, turning them over halfway through.

Remove the pan from the oven and drizzle over the honey. Return to the oven and continue to cook for 15 to 20 minutes, basting occasionally with the honey and juices in the pan, until golden brown, sticky, and thoroughly cooked. To check, pierce the thickest part of the drumstick with a skewer; the juices should run clear. If there is any sign of pink, continue to cook for a few minutes more. If in doubt, cut through one of the drumsticks to the bone to check.

Remove the chicken from the oven and drain well before serving.

MINI BREADED MEATBALLS

I can guarantee that these homemade meatballs, served with oven-baked potato wedges and real tomato ketchup, will go down a treat at any children's party

PREPARATION TIME
12–15 minutes, plus 30 minutes chilling time
COOKING TIME 12–15 minutes

1–2 slices day-old whole-wheat bread

1 recipe Beef Burgers (page 106)

1 tablespoon whole-wheat flour

1 large egg, beaten

to serve

Salsa (page 96)

reduced-calorie mayonnaise

low-fat fromage frais mixed with chopped fresh herbs

20 toothpicks

makes 20 balls

Cut the bread into small strips. Put them in a blender or food processor and blend briefly to make bread crumbs. Transfer to a shallow dish.

Prepare the Beef Burger mixture as directed on page 106. Use clean hands to shape the mixture into about 20 even balls about the size of an apricot (a perfect job for little hands).

Put the flour on a plate and the beaten egg in a shallow dish. Roll the balls in the flour until well coated, then dip them in the egg, shaking off any excess. Roll them in the bread crumbs until evenly coated and transfer to a large plate. Cover and chill in the refrigerator for at least 30 minutes.

Put the meatballs in a nonstick roasting pan and cook in a preheated oven at 400°F for 12 to 15 minutes, turning the balls occasionally, until golden brown and crisp.

Put a toothpick in each meatball and transfer to a large serving plate. Serve warm, accompanied by dipping sauces, such as salsa, mayonnaise, or herby fromage frais.

COOK'S TIP
- These meatballs would make a great pasta dish. Prepare the Tomato Sauce for Pasta (page 86), add the meatballs to the sauce, and heat thoroughly. Serve on top of freshly cooked, hot pasta.

CUPCAKES

Storebought cupcakes are a mixture of white flour, saturated fat, sugar, and colored icing, which may contain additives known to cause behavioral problems. These avoid unnecessary additives by using white icing and naturally colored cherries and the sugar content is kept low by adding orange juice.

PREPARATION TIME 15 minutes
COOKING TIME 15–20 minutes

½ cup self-rising flour

½ cup whole-wheat flour

2 teaspoons baking powder

½ teaspoon baking soda

½ cup unrefined granulated sugar

6 tablespoons sunflower oil

2 eggs, beaten

¼ cup freshly squeezed orange juice

1 cup confectioners' sugar

naturally colored glacé cherries, to decorate

a 12-hole muffin pan, lined with 12 paper liners

makes 12

Sift the flours, baking powder, and baking soda into a large bowl and stir in the sugar. Using a wooden spoon or hand-held electric beater, gradually beat in the oil and then the eggs until the mixture is smooth and creamy. Add 1 tablespoon orange juice and mix gently to give a soft, dropping consistency. If the mixture feels too stiff, add a little more orange juice.

Spoon the mixture into the paper liners, filling them about three-quarters full. Bake in a preheated oven at 350°F for 15 to 20 minutes until golden and firm to the touch. Remove from the oven and let cool.

Sift the confectioners' sugar into a bowl. Add the remaining orange juice and mix until smooth. Spoon over the tops of the cooled cakes. Let set slightly, then decorate with the cherries. Best eaten within 2 days.

VARIATION
• Instead of the cherries, use good quality grated chocolate to decorate.

DOUBLE CHOCOLATE FRUITY SQUARES

PREPARATION TIME 15 minutes, plus 2 hours chilling time

6½ oz. semisweet chocolate (at least 70 percent cocoa solids)

7 tablespoons sunflower margarine

2 tablespoons freshly squeezed orange juice

about 6 low-fat English digestive biscuits

2 oz. good quality white chocolate

¼ cup raisins

⅓ cup dried apricots, chopped

¼ cup dried cherries or cranberries

a baking pan, 8 inches square, lightly greased

makes 16 squares

Break the semisweet chocolate into small squares and put them in a heavy-based saucepan with the margarine and orange juice. Heat gently for 3 to 4 minutes, stirring occasionally, until melted. Stir until smooth.

Crush the biscuits in a food processor or put them in a plastic bag and crush with a rolling pin. Roughly chop the white chocolate. Add the crushed cookies, white chocolate, and all the dried fruit to the melted chocolate mixture. Stir well so all the ingredients are lightly coated with chocolate.

Spoon into the prepared pan and press down lightly with the back of a wooden spoon. Transfer to the refrigerator and let set for at least 2 hours. Cut into squares, to serve. Store lightly covered in the refrigerator for up to 4 days.

VARIATION
• Replace this selection of dried fruit with others of your choice, such as raisins or mango, and add some finely chopped nuts, if desired.

CHOCOLATE-DIPPED FRUIT

There is nothing wrong with letting your children eat chocolate from time to time, especially if it is used to coat fresh fruit as it is here. Kids will love helping to make these.

PREPARATION TIME 10–15 minutes, plus 1 hour setting time

1 lb. fresh, ripe, but firm fruit, such as strawberries, apples, seedless grapes, or satsumas

6½ oz. semisweet chocolate (at least 70 percent cocoa solids), broken into pieces

1 teaspoon golden syrup

a few toothpicks or skewers

serves 4

Wash the fruit and dry it carefully with paper towels. Leave the small fruit whole. Cut the apples into thin wedges and remove the core. Divide the satsumas into segments.

Put the chocolate and golden syrup in a heatproof bowl. Place the bowl over a saucepan of gently simmering, not boiling, water, making sure the base of the bowl doesn't come into contact with the water. Heat gently, stirring occasionally, until the chocolate is melted and smooth. Remove the bowl from the heat and let cool slightly.

Pierce a piece of fruit with a toothpick or skewer and dip it into the melted chocolate. Transfer to a sheet of nonstick parchment paper and let set for about 1 hour. Eat within 3 to 4 hours of coating.

FROZEN FRUIT POPS

These pops are a real summer treat for kids and they are full of fresh fruit or freshly squeezed fruit juice.

PREPARATION TIME 5–10 minutes
FREEZING TIME 2–3 hours

2½ cups freshly squeezed fruit juice, such as orange, apple or pineapple juice or 2 pints fresh ripe fruit, such as strawberries, raspberries, or a mixture of both

3–4 tablespoons superfine sugar (optional)

8 frozen treat molds

makes 8 pops

Set the freezer to rapid freeze. Rinse out the molds with cold water.

If using fruit juice, carefully pour the juice into the moulds, then push the handle tops into the pops.

If using fresh ripe fruit, remove any stalks, rinse lightly, and cut any large fruit in half. Put the fruit in a saucepan, add sugar to taste, and ⅔ cup water. Cook over gentle heat for 5 minutes or until the fruit has collapsed. Let cool slightly, then transfer to a food processor or blender and process to form a puree. Push the puree through a fine, non-metallic strainer to remove the pips.

Make the puree up to 2⅓ cups with filtered water or freshly squeezed orange juice. Pour it into the treat molds, then push a handle top into each pop.

Freeze for at least 4 hours until frozen. Use within 2 to 3 days.

VARIATION
* Fill the treat molds with milk shake (page 71) or one of the smoothies on page 42, and freeze as above.

CHOCOLATE & RASPBERRY BIRTHDAY CAKE

Although this recipe contains cream, it doesn't require the butter used in most cakes. The refined white flour is also absent and instead it uses protein-packed almonds to give a far healthier treat for a child's birthday.

PREPARATION TIME 20 minutes
COOKING TIME 25–30 minutes

4 eggs

¾ cup unrefined granulated sugar

3½ oz. semisweet chocolate (at least 70 percent cocoa solids), broken into small pieces

1 cup ground almonds

⅔ cup heavy cream or créme fraîche

8–10 oz. fresh raspberries

2 small cake pans, 6 inches diameter, lightly greased and lined with parchment paper

serves 8

Put the eggs and sugar in a heatproof bowl and place over a saucepan of gently simmering water. Beat with a hand-held electric beater for 5 to 8 minutes until very thick and creamy. The mixture should leave a trail when it drips from the beaters. Remove the bowl from the saucepan and beat for another 3 to 5 minutes until cool.

Put the chocolate in a small heatproof bowl and place it over a saucepan of gently simmering, not boiling, water, making sure that the base of the bowl doesn't come into contact with the water. Heat gently until the chocolate has melted. Remove the bowl from the saucepan and stir the chocolate until smooth. Let cool.

Gradually add the cooled chocolate to the beaten egg mixture, stirring gently. Stir in the ground almonds, mixing lightly. Divide the mixture evenly between the 2 sandwich pans, tap each pan lightly on the counter to remove any air bubbles.

Bake in a preheated oven at 350°F for 25 to 30 minutes until well risen and the tops spring back when touched lightly with your finger. Remove from the oven and let the cakes cool in the pans for about 10 minutes before transferring them to a wire cooling rack to cool completely. The surface will crisp up and crack as it cools. Remove and discard the parchment paper.

Beat the cream, if using, with a hand-held electric beater until soft peaks form. Spread half the cream or crème fraîche over one layer of the cake and top with half the raspberries. Put the second cake layer on top and decorate with the remaining cream or crème fraîche and raspberries. Store lightly covered in the refrigerator until required. The undecorated cake will keep for 2 days.

VARIATION
• For an alternative birthday cake idea, make the Easy Carrot Cupcakes on page 64. Put a slice of banana on top of each one (held in place with some lemon cream cheese icing) to act as a birthday candle holder, then carefully stack the cakes on a plate, pyramid-style. Light the candles when ready. This works particularly well for younger children because each child can have their own cake and get a chance to blow out the candles. They are easy to put in party bags, too.

INDEX

author's acknowledgments

My biggest thank you has to go to my two adorable little boys, Barney and Brook, not only for inspiring me to write this book in the first place, but for reminding me on a daily basis just how important it is to serve our next generation the very best food we possibly can. Thanks also to Louis, for being the best husband and dad (ever!). Last, but by no means least, I'd like to thank all of the brilliant team at Ryland Peters & Small, especially Sharon Cochrane and Alison Starling, and Gina Steer.

FEEDBACK

If you have any feedback about any of the recipes or issues in this book, or if you require further information about healthy eating for kids, please visit www.realfoodforkids.com or email me at r.a.hill@realfoodforkids.com.

publisher's acknowledgments

The publisher would like to thank the adorable models, Christina, Darla, Ellie, Elliot, Eve, Gaia, Georgina, Gregory, Hassia, Havana, Sammy, and Thomas. A special thank you also goes to their parents.